The Idea of Ideas

THE **IDEA** OF IDEAS

BY ROBERT W. GALVIN

MOTOROLA UNIVERSITY PRESS
SCHAUMBURG, ILLINOIS
1991

Published by Motorola University Press.

Typeset in Perpetua
by Paul Baker Typography Inc.,
Evanston, Illinois.
Printing and binding by Kingsport Press,
Kingsport, Tennessee.

Cover: Mohawk Artemis, Navy Blue;
End sheets: Rainbow Felt Gray;
Text stock: Lindenmeyer Sebago, Eggshell.

Design by Hayward Blake & Company,
Evanston, Illinois.
Illustration on page 6 by Noli Novak.
Quotation on cover by Robert W. Galvin.

ISBN: 1-56946-002-7

The IDEA of IDEAS

TABLE OF CONTENTS

INTRODUCTION

"....my father treated me to the most demanding discipline. He trusted me!"

BOB GALVIN

Paul V. Galvin on the left and Robert W. Galvin at right

Expectation, and Influencing Factors

The idea of this book is ideas. Ideas that have shaped the destiny of Motorola. It acclaims the role of others' ideas. It details the role of some of my ideas. It challenges the expectation level of idea creation.

This book is neither a biography nor a career story. It is a litany of ideas that made some difference and other circumstances where the absence of ideas found us wanting. It is a personal account because ideas are the product of people.

Thousands of people have enriched Motorola's service and growth, and these have been acclaimed in countless ways through the 50-plus years that I have witnessed these remarkable contributions. Hundreds and hundreds of people have made extraordinary contributions with ideas that have had leverage impact on the affairs of the institution.

In the course of compiling the contents of this book, I asked each of the affected officers of the company to list in topic sentence form five ideas each contributed which most satisfied the officer and five more ideas by others which each particularly admired. The brilliance and influence of most of them were inspiring to recall. I only wish it were practical to detail in a text such as this each of these leading thoughts.

With all that all have contributed, and with what I have contributed, I have long been of the mind that our expectation level is too little compared to what is contributable. I have learned enough about the potential for developing one's creative skills to believe that we can, in the era ahead, train ourselves and commit ourselves to a step function improvement to greater creativity. It is my desire that by going to school on this anthology of personal experience, successes and failures, dealing with the creation and the employment of true and new "do differentlies" that our company will multiply its creativity and thus its service and effectiveness to society.

Certain pivotal factors have influenced my interest in ideation. Although I have not catalogued each of the following in the chronology with which they may have impacted me, each of these became a significant input in that period of my life prior to my having become 30 years of age.

I remember early on hearing various people and reading various authors who refer to that apparent common wisdom that if a manager could account for 55% to 60% of his decisions being right that this would lead to the success of his institution. To this day, I hear an occasional reference to that representation. From the beginning I questioned that proposition. My thought process may not have been very profound but somehow a grade of 80 or 90 had been ingrained in my mind as being the more passing grade. Paradoxically, I even wondered, if a leader could come up with just one extraordinary right decision once in a while, wouldn't that unto itself be justification for the leadership qualities of that individual? But what I really found myself questioning was whether or not the function of decision making was necessarily the first order of importance. I had learned that there were two cerebral functions — judgment and creativity — and although the process of creativity was vague to me then, I kept wondering whether there wasn't at least a co-equal importance and, thus, I assigned a conscious curiosity to test my instincts. I later came to the realization that I could not be confident of the best decision without the optimum choices (ideas) from which to choose.

In the early course of that curiosity a book came to my attention by Alex Osborn, a principal of the advertising firm of Batten, Barton, Durstine and Osborn, a distinguished advertising agency. The book was titled *Your Creative Power*. As I studied it, I discovered that it was a simple description of the vocational skills acquirable if one aspired to being purposefully creative. Later, I will reference the common sense that the Osborn book and other resources provided.

About that same time an old high school friend of mine shared his copy of a biography of Bernard Baruch, a preeminent investment banker and advisor to presidents in the early third of the century. I was fascinated with the breadth and variety of Baruch's talents and contribution to business and public affairs. The most critical message that came out of this story to me was Baruch's basic advocacy that if the crowd is going one way, be curious as to whether you might better go the opposite. He first seemed to apply this thinking to the psychology of investors in the stock market. But one could distill from so many other of his experiences in life that he had a propensity to ask whether the opposite of whatever was the more conventional thought or mode of the day could be the worthy direction one could pursue. That struck me as a valuable test. Further, if I was to find merit in challenging the common wisdom, then clearly I was going to have to offer some value-added in consideration of doing a different or opposite thing than the conventional direction was to suggest.

On a different subject, my mother stimulated my interest and skills in elocution. My father was a role model as a public spokesman. I developed an interest in public speaking and debate. My debate coach at Notre Dame taught our team the ultimate lesson for public speaking and communicating. "The essence of a good speech," he said, "is having something to say." I came to learn that meant more than just repeating the facts that were known or available. It meant providing the fresh look and the new extension of what was available. It meant providing the fresh look and the new extension of what was conversable.

Also, I was stimulated by my father's frequent reference to a "healthy spirit of discontent." Although most often positive and always appreciative, he was constantly looking for the inadequate or the imperfect. But to deal with this in simply a negative and challenging way was insufficient to him. He knew that he had to contribute something positive to turn that discontent to something that was acceptable.

Each of these insights leaned in the direction that there was an obligation and a responsibility to find ways of contributing fresh approaches and fresh answers. The importance of creativity began to dawn early.

There is an additional value that fits among the influencing factors that stirred my interest in the creative. It is a fundamental unto itself and is essential to creativity. It is best introduced by anecdote.

I often take my place before university classes and assemblies, sharing experiences with students. More often than not I am asked, "You have referenced the important contributions of your father as the founder and early leader of your company. Is there any one thing that you can point to that your father instilled in you as your motivation?"

"Yes," I reply, "my father treated me to the most demanding discipline. He trusted me!"

This is the highest respect that one person can give to another. It is the most demanding motivator. One does not dare let the other person down.

In my earlier years I did not fully appreciate what my father had imparted. It was only in my middle and later years that I came to the recognition and appreciation of that which he vested.

What is the relevance of that to the prioritization of creative thinking as a prime responsibility?

One's creativity depends on interaction with others —
others one trusts — others who feel trusted. For one to be
unfettered in risking creative interaction with another, that
other must know the trust of openness, objectivity and a
complementary creative spirit. Inherent to this, in order to
trust, one must be trustable. Trust is a power. The power to
trust and be trusted is an essential and inherent prerequisite quality to the optimum development and employment
of a creative culture.

So, building on the base of the natural level of creativity of many people and the need for optimum choices,
fresh answers to discontents as well as really having something (new) to say, I discerned promise in acquiring
vocational skills, questioning the conventional and nurturing a trusting environment aimed at enhancing creativity —
personally and corporately.

In the essays that follow, my or "our" thinking on
various and related subjects is revealed. In some instances
they represent original ways of reflecting on old ideas.
In others, they express actual originality or significant
variations from the expected or the conventional. In total,
they manifest some of the different reasons we in Motorola
are who and why we are.

THE IDEA PROCESS:
ITS ROLE

"Be in motion for motion's sake."
PAUL GALVIN

Creativity: Our Latent Power

All of us are naturally curious and imaginative. We manifest these qualities particularly as children. Education inadequacies and disciplines, family direction and control, and traditional work ethics suppress them. Thus, for most adults creative juices languish.

My instinct about them sustained. Yet, I had no manifest skill. I read many things about creativity that happened my way but I did not have the initiative to delve purposefully into the subject as a youth.

Then, good fortune struck. I read a short review about a new book (circa 1950) written by a man I respected but did not know, Alex Osborn. He was a distinguished partner in the advertising agency Batten, Barton, Durstine and Osborn.

The book: *Your Creative Power*. I sent for it. I devoured it. It became one of two vocational books that immensely shaped my approach to most situations, problems and opportunities. The two books so complemented each other that their combined effect was revolutionary to me.

The other book, a biography of Bernard Baruch, questioned following the crowd. It urged: dare to go a different way, think differently.

Alex Osborn, similarly in part, described the unworthy obvious: most of us leap to conclusions, turn off the ideas of others and are rebuffed too often as we offer our ideas. Those are our conventional ways. I vowed to do otherwise. That's what he taught.

Osborn's book is a primer. It simply tells how, as well as why, to be creative. It persuaded me I could learn to do it. It worked. I believe everyone can learn to be much more creative and that it is essential. I even suggested that idea to eminent educators. As you would suspect, they knew better!

I've since learned there are many such books. Some may be superior. But altogether they have been too little heeded. As a result, we adults perceive ourselves primarily as decision makers, yet we rarely search for an adequate selection of choices (ideas) from which to better judge.

I have lived a full professional life with exceptional people. Their creativity abounds. But the highest compliment I can pay to all of us is to acclaim our even greater potential at idea generation and the even better judgments that will follow.

As is accounted for elsewhere in this book, we in our company thought we were tops in quality at an earlier time only to learn there were dramatically better ways. Our expectations and processes then were embarrassingly low. We changed directions for the good.

I am convinced that the potential exists for a "c" change — a cerebral change — a creativity change throughout some institution like Motorola which can further set the institution apart from its contemporaries and competitors.

That is the idea of this essay — virtual universal commitment to learning better how to be more creative hourly, daily. We can and should apply consciously, confidently, purposely and frequently, the simpler, satisfying, appropriate steps to create more and then better ideas.

Osborn's methods are similar to others. He describes the creative process in two general steps: hunt up the facts, change what you find.

We inherently possess many facts: first-hand experiences, hard knocks, travel, love, grief, reading, studies, etc. We can add to that fuel so much more that we hunt up. How?

Set a target. Segment, break down the issue or problem. Fill in the facts.

Then ask questions. Endless questions. Crazy questions. What can we add, subtract, combine, adopt, and so on.

Create a check list. Go back over the process.

Aim for quantity. **Quantity!** Ignore quality early on.

If one has been thrust into a problem requiring immediate ideas then one's energies aimed at trying to be creative are automatically called for. Even then we are often lacking.

More often than not, self-starting is obliged to generate ideas. So the effective creative thinker sets a time and place to create; sets a quota (a quantity) of ideas to be conceived and a deadline. The best thinkers will team up. When they do, they insist on the most stimulating, affirmative and inspiring environment. This demands a total deferral of judgment. **Don't judge too soon!**

Write, display, illustrate the ideas. Association follows so much easier.

Fun? Yes! Easy? Rarely! Discouragements must be overcome. Sustained drive is essential. All of the above will take perseverance, perspiration. Organized, flexible thinking is required. That's hard work.

Fortunately, creative power is developable. Like any skill and at any age, with exercise each of us can become noticeably more competent. Games like chess, Twenty Questions, charades, are helpful exercises. So are puzzles, quizzes and hobbies. Writing is excellent and so is public speaking. Or making up fantasies for the kids. But **actual doing is the best!**

The rewards are so valuable. The problem is we haven't come close to demonstrating our full value, the latent creative power within us.

LEADERSHIP

"*Spread hope.*"

GENERAL DORIOT,
AMERICAN RESEARCH AND DEVELOPMENT

"*At times we must engage an act of faith that key things are doable that are not provable.*"

BOB GALVIN

The Paradox of Leadership

This is a special selective idea of leadership. It finds its
expression in a series of paradoxes.

We know so much about leadership, yet we know too
little. We can define it in general but find it hard to partic-
ularize. We recognize it when obvious, but it is not always
obvious why. We practice leadership, which implies we are
still preparing for the real thing.

It is neither necessary to impress on you an elaborate
definition of leadership nor is this an appropriate time to
characterize its many styles. Let it suffice that we acknowledge that no leader is worthy of the title absent creative
and judgmental intelligence, courage, heart, spirit, integrity
and vision applied to the accomplishment of a purposeful
result through the efforts of followers and the leader.
Rather, I elect to share with you some observations on a
further series of paradoxes that reveal themselves as we
analyze leadership.

~

When one is vested with the role of leader, he inherits more freedom. The power of leadership endows him with rights to a greater range of self-determination of his own destiny. It is he who may determine the what or the how and the when or the where of important events.

Yet, as with all rights, there is a commensurate, balancing group of responsibilities that impose upon his freedom. The leader cannot avoid the act of determining the what or the who or the where. He cannot avoid being prepared to make these determinations. He cannot avoid seeing to their implementation. He cannot avoid living with the consequences of his decision on others and the demands these consequences impose on him. Only time will prove the merit of his stewardship. Because he is driven to pass this test of time he will be obliged often to serve others more than himself. This obligation will more and more circumscribe his destiny. So those who assume true leadership will wonder from time to time if the apparent freedom of the leader adds a greater measure of independence, or whether the dependence of others on him restricts his own freedom.

~

For one to lead implies that others follow. But is the leader a breed apart, or is she rather the better follower? Leadership casts the leader in many such roles:

Observer *of the work her associates perform*
Senser *of attitudes, feelings and trends*
Listener *to ideas, suggestions and complaints*
Student *of advisors, inside and outside her institution*
Product *of experience, both hers and others'*
Mimic *of other leaders who have earned her respect*

Is she not the better follower, as she learns more quickly and surely from the past, selects the correct advice and trends, chooses the simpler work patterns and combines the best of other leaders? Is it not good leadership to know when not to follow an aimless path?

The paradox again: to lead well presumes the ability to follow smartly.

~

Because a leader is human and fallible, his and her leadership is in one sense finite — constrained by mortality and human imperfections. In another sense the leader's influence is almost limitless.

He and she can spread hope, lend courage, kindle confidence, impart knowledge, give heart, instill spirit, elevate standards, display vision, set direction, and call for action today and each tomorrow.

The frequency with which one can perform these leadership functions seems without measure. His and her effectiveness and personal resources, rather than attenuating with use, amplify as he and she reuse and extend the skills.

Like the tree whose shadow falls where the tree is not,

the consequence of the leader's act radiates beyond the fondest perception.

Again we see the paradox of the leader — a finite person with an apparent infinite influence.

~

A leader is decisive, is called on to make many critical choices, and can thrive on the power and the attention of that decision-making role. Yet the leader of leaders moves progressively away from that role.

Yes, he or she can be decisive and command as required. Yet that leader's prime responsibility is not to decide or direct but to create and maintain an evocative situation, stimulating an atmosphere of objective participation, keeping the goal in sight, recognizing valid consensus, inviting unequivocal recommendation and finally vesting increasingly in others the privilege to learn through their own decisions.

A wiser man put it thus: "We measure the effectiveness of the true leader not in terms of the leadership he exercises but in terms of the leadership he evokes; not in terms of his power over others, but in terms of the power he releases in others; not in terms of the goals he sets and the directions he gives but in terms of the plans of action others work out for themselves with his help; not in terms of decisions made, events completed and the inevitable success and growth that follow from such released energy but in terms of growth in competence, sense of responsibility and in personal satisfaction among many participants.

Under this kind of leadership it may not always be clear at any given moment just who is leading. Nor is this important. What is important is that others are learning to lead well."

The complement to that paradox is that the growth that such leadership stimulates generates an ever-growing institution and an ever-increasing number of critical choices, more than enough of which fall squarely back on the shoulders of the leader who trained and willingly shared decision making with others.

~

And there are others which, if not paradoxes, at least are incongruities. Have we not witnessed some who have claimed leadership yet never fully achieved it? Have we not observed others who have shunned leadership only to have it thrust upon them?

Each of us is at once part leader and part follower as we play our roles in life. Fortunately there is a spark of leadership quality in many men and women, and most fortunately the flame of future leadership burns brightly in many. It is this wellspring from which we will draw and which gives us confidence for the continued advance of society.

Walter Lippmann once observed: "The final test of a leader is that he leaves behind in other men the conviction and will to carry on."

The Renewal of Leadership

On the occasion of the dedication of the Corporation's new training center on May 6, 1986, the following was the dedication statement:

The singling out of renewal is not creative unto itself. But the constant quest for renewal demands it.

Today we dedicate this education center to the renewal of leadership. The Center will speak for itself as a statement of leadership renewing.

This is the second dedication of a Motorola corporate educational institution. The first was in the far distant and prophetically named town of Oracle, Arizona, years ago. We dedicated that Executive Institute to leadership. The words* spoken there are inscribed and alive. They are a creed.

Today we rededicate ourselves to the renewal of leadership.

*See *The Paradox of Leadership*: Page 25

The Chief Executive Office has spoken of that word —
renewal — with recent emphasis to all the management of
the corporation. The context was: The Company Vision —
with the process of timely renewal noted as the most
driving force to open and sharpen our visioning competence, aimed at determining the company we will always
be striving to be.

In that talk we asked every leader to conjure the multifaceted meanings and powers of the word renewal.

This forum provides the natural coincidence to personally do the same.

Renewal is blood brother to change. Change unto itself
is essential. But, taken alone: it is limited. It customarily
implies inevitability; even an insufficient ability to cope
with some changing events. It seems to suggest most everything has to be different. It does not sufficiently suggest an
original start as if there is not yet something to change.

Yes, renewal is change. It calls for "do differently." It is
willing to replace and redo. But it also cherishes the proven
basics. It is capable of founding anew.

Let's square this interpretation of renewal by picturing
its four sides.

1. At the base: Keep the right things the same. Renewal
    means reconfirming our dedication to proven values and
    roots; returning to the original state when change is
    second best; and repeating, doing again what was rightly
    done before.

2. *On the one side: Do differently, of course, frequently, timely. Train, change for the better, steadily, consistently. Rejuvenate to restore youthful vigor. Extend, contract as a need is anticipated. Redo so extensively as to make like new.*

3. *On the other side: Be willing and able to begin again. Be capable of being replaced. Note that last statement is positive — be capable of being replaced. The enlightened renewer will not countenance being the victim of replacement by someone else's technology or talent. Rather, he or she will anticipate, learn and lead with the alternates and substitutes — adding to or replacing our something old with our something new.*

4. *At the top — the toughest of all renewals: Begin an original. Refound. Start up.*

Each of these is a major call to action. Collectively they are an awesome responsibility.

Each of us and all the other individuals we represent must take ownership of our share of these acts of renewal. Prepare for them. Reach out to them. Stand up for them.

What we are saying again here is that renewal in all of its dimensions is a pointedly personal privilege and duty.

It's yours.

It's mine.

Just as it was Paul Galvin's.

He is recalled to us today as we impart his name, so appropriately, to this continuing education center.

He was the original teacher.

His lessons are ever more valid.

He was the restless renewer.

He renewed in every way.

He was the driving force.

It was his most driving force.

Certain of our associates originally asked that my name be applied singularly here. I was more than reluctant as this is our institution. Then we thought to couple mine to his. That idea then took on a rare and appreciated distinction. I acceded, but primarily because of the symbolism of father to son — the master demonstration of mankind's requirement to renew.

He did instill the spirit in me. I will not shy from that claim.

But what he would want is that the torch I hold high in his image will fire each of our spirits to emblazon our business realm with constant glowing and growing achievements by ever abler, ever smarter peers and associates who will spark our continuous renewal.

The Importance of Being an Officer

When I was a youngster in the company I was aware of the fact that there were 8 or 9 officials who had officer titles. I recognized that these men were talented and deserving. As time went on I wondered about the next-to-be officer. I became, in effect, a student of the issue. Where is that dividing line between someone who becomes an officer and someone who has not yet attained that position?

During that early observation period there were infrequent changes. After I gained some experience, it seemed that a certain additional man was deserving. He was the head accountant. He reported to the Vice President and Chief Financial Officer. Al, the head accountant, was capable and constantly in demand. The Chief Financial Officer was also ably performing. Both accounting seniors' leadership was vital to our small Corporation.

I began to quietly raise the question, "Shouldn't Al be a vice president?" There was inherent resistance. Those who were already officers had a subliminal barrier. Somehow, once they became officers it was hard to imagine that the next person was their equal. Then there was the puzzling numbers question. Would we be spreading officers too far and therefore too thin and reducing the distinction of the importance of officerships?

I persisted in my quiet query and eventual advocacy to my father and other officers even though I was not an officer or close to being an officer candidate. Not long afterward, Al Arnold was named a vice president. Whether he would have been named a vice president only a few more months later without my campaigning, or for that matter, whether he would have been named an officer earlier if I had kept quiet on the subject, I'll never know. But the experience of dealing with the officership nomination and selection was becoming an education unto itself.

In the early years to come, because our company was small enough, I always knew the potential candidates for officers as well as anyone else. I tried to move in the vanguard of an advocate of their ascendancy to the higher role when their conduct and competences had reached the appropriate level. Inevitably, at each stage of the next list of candidates to be considered, there would be automatic resistance by many incumbents. Were we watering down the importance of officers? Were we creating the wrong image by having too many officers? Was this structurally sound?, etc.

At any given level of size of comparing our company to most any other similar business, we progressively moved to where we had a significantly larger number of officers than comparable companies. From two, to as many as five times more. Many is the time that my senior officer associates have wrung their hands over whether that was the right thing to do. But we persisted and the next time around we would deliberate and mostly continue on our more liberal approach. Later I came to explain the issue over-simply — "If a man or woman looks like an officer, then let's call that person an officer." With it all, our standards were and are extremely high.

Over the period circa 1950 to 1990, when I was over-seeing this process, we made infrequent mistakes. But for every one that might have been promoted over his or her head, a hundred assumed responsibility with great enthusiasm and alacrity.

This idea of liberal officer appointment is distinctive in appearance and in conduct. Time will tell whether the long term consequences net the most favorable results to our Corporation. It's worked well so far. Most of our compatriots in industry are more conservative in this regard. They are running successful companies. We are no less successful currently with our large number of officers. At some point in time, it is conceivable that the fact that we have this culture and practice will prove to be an even more distinctive competence of our institution.

Why shouldn't many people be officers of a large corporation? Comparatively, if they were working for small corporations they would be officers doing the excellent work that they are doing here. I was bred on the essentiality of some 8 or 9 officers in our little ten million dollar company back in 1940. I watch among the excellent small companies and note that there are from 5 to 10 officers in other small companies today. That evidence hardly dictates one officer per million of sales. But a liberal standard should not be ignored.

Motorola is a series of many businesses; some moderate in size. Most take officer quality people to lead.

We speak of treating people with respect and dignity; doing so in accordance with their individual needs and accomplishments. It is my idea that if an individual in a company the size and the growth potentials of ours has the qualities of officership and has the responsibilities of officership, then he or she dearly deserves that regard and recognition.

It is true that with an officership goes some moderate perquisite. This is a cost. But the value to the company, gained as a function of the recognition and the motivation, is deserving and more than worth it.

Fortunately, most of these able appointees reach out to grow even more as a result of that acknowledgement and authority. More and more have grown to the stature of major leadership. That leadership is essential to the ongoing growth and quality service of an aspiring institution.

The Equal Differences
Among Those at the Top

As I have moved through the myriad stages of factory, lab and sales assignments, supervising, directing, managing and leading within the company; as I have observed and admired the multiple contributions of my able associates, I have concluded that those at the top engage in three classes of activities. The first of these is Running a Business. The second is Managing the Corporation. The third is Leading the Institution.

These are three co-equal experiences in importance. It is worth understanding the difference. In fact, it is essential. It is worth understanding that most of us may or can do at least some parts of all three; that each requires separate focus in their time; that at times we are doing all three simultaneously, although with selective emphasis.

Running a business is often considered the most fun of all the experiences that one has through the stages of a career in a corporation. It's the hands on, direct authority, visible consequence class of job. It's the cherished line authority, results measurable, profit accountable activity. It's the frontline association with the discovery of a market, the designing and providing for the market, the dealing with the customer, the winning or the losing on a day-to-day basis. Many who have had that experience resist giving it up even when promoted. As a matter of fact, once promoted, many of us become a problem to those who inherit our recent authority to run the business. We hanker to revisit it — to call its shots again.

Managing the company takes in the whole — all the businesses, all the general functions. Those cast in that role are accountable for the whole but not readily or in totality accountable for its parts. These managers are responsible for raising resources and resource apportionment and support which, incidentally, may favor certain businesses and functions. That choice helps determine the optimizing (or otherwise) of the company's overall return on investment and business-by-business growth rate, market share, people's development and earnings rate. The manager of the company must be creator, judge and jury, facilitator, coordinator, tone setter, driver, spokesman, problem spotter, problem solving coach, keeper of the faith, culture guardian, standard setter, doer and role model to all. The list can go on.

It is not close to the purpose of this book to be the definitive text on managing the corporation. Rather, this short essay only wishes to heighten the realization that in all of its readily discoverable dimensions, managing the corporation is and should be very different than running one of its businesses. The incumbents should act accordingly. The managers of the corporation must work the hardest at this both by learning the real worth of what should be their critical value added and the concomitant conduct of getting out of the way of the runners of businesses who with considerable independence must be, or become, able to maximize the service to and results from that business's customer satisfaction.

Managing the corporation, which is so important, implies guidance aimed at increasing success in the company's apparent, generic, naturally evolving configuration with certain generally agreed to, although flexible, ways, means and targets. The managers of the corporation must also see outside that scope into their dual role of periodically leading the institution elsewhere.

Realization of, knowledge about and expectations concerning the leading of the institution — the third of the classes of activities — is a magnet that can attract the manager of the corporation away from excessive reflection on and involvement in particular favorite businesses. It can fire a new excitement and expectation in job content and expanded results. It can shape the corporation into a far better or different institution for profit.

Leading the institution means taking it somewhere else for the better. The word "somewhere" will only incidentally and occasionally involve geography. In this special context it assumes a virtual limitlessness of dimension. It can pursue the most detailed or the broadest derivatives of the why, the what, and the how of a better or best new.

The ultimate consequence of the questioning and imagination of this leader will lift much of, if not the entire, institution almost simultaneously to a heightened level. As a result of a major do differently, the company may literally become a very different entity. The corporation may even become a more manageable institution.

No, we're not talking about a rare need to convert a food merchant, for example, into a steel mill or yesterday's definition of restructuring. Rather, we're envisioning step function enhancements of or totally new key values or processes; substantially different emphasis on functions or standards; attention to virtually ignored issues; clearly better anticipations; major, gutsy commitments; switching from inward to outward lookings; or something as seemingly unimportant as becoming better listeners.

The role of leader of the institution can also be joined by key professionals with exceptional qualities in their day-to-day field. I particularly refer to those not yet enrobed with a fancy title or high organization structure standing. Often these professionals are the first with the competence of a vision of some over-the-horizon opportunity. This is a particularly true and possible potential from broad-gauged engineers and scientists. But others, like marketing folk, can hatch promising product and systems visions also. Or personnel professionals may sense a fundamental trend with and for people. And so on. There are past and present examples of fruitful results from those high competence professionals' wise anticipation and commitment to fundamentally new directions.

There cannot be an isolated, narrowly assigned job position called Leader of the Institution. For one to contribute to that objective one must be current with business and corporate level affairs. So too, for one to hold promise of broadening beyond a "Running the Business" official and a "Managing the Corporation" officer, one must be an ever-increasing contributor to the institutional renewal role.

But will there be enough candidates and contributors? Will every meritorious initiative of theirs be heard receptively and encouraged appropriately? Will the "Runners" be so busy running that they cut the others off? Will the "Managers" be so preoccupied that they are devoting too little time to listening to and supporting those others whose visionary advocacies make the "Leader" part of the manager's job optimally double?

The Runner of a business, the Manager of the corporation, have their direct, personal, principal job to do, of course. Yet, each of them has a simultaneous obligation to be personally within earshot and receptive to the pivotable visionary nominations that percolate from the professionals around them. In fact it must be their obligation to stimulate this additional valuable role — Leading the institution.

Succession

Early on, my father was obsessed with management succession. Ironically, he did not fear his own demise. His concern was for the company.

He could hardly wait to place me in a pivotal position to deal with such an unpredictable possibility. Fortunately, he lived to near a conventional retirement age confident then that his succession concerns were relieved.

My instincts were never so intense. But I was ever mindful. So, within a short time following my assumption of senior leadership in 1959, and with the full involvement of the Board of Directors, we saw to the elevation and addition of one talented pair of Chief Executive Office team members following another in natural timely order. The distinguished team of Elmer Wavering and Dan Noble joined me in the office in the '60s and early '70s. Bill Weisz, and later John Mitchell, phased in capably in the '70s and '80s. There was always a private but clear understanding of succession hierarchy. We were prepared for unscheduleable change throughout that quarter of a century. Of course, that was but one of the reasons for the office of three. The principal reasons were the leadership to be contributed and the work load to be borne.

Blessed with good health, the prospect for my serving to a natural retirement date at sixty-five or so years of age appeared likely as the '80s unfolded. The calendar turned to mid-1983. It was time for fresh ideas. A purposely planable and executable succession was now in order.

Bill Weisz, then Vice Chairman and Chief Operating Officer, and John Mitchell, then President and Assistant Chief Operating Officer, were eminently qualified to carry on. Their role in our office had been performed exemplarily. That office, our office, had successfully served most of its expected time.

We were contemporaries. There were just a couple of years difference between Bill's and my age and a similar difference between Bill and John. By the time a conventionally timed turnover of responsibility would be consummated involving me, all of us would be in our sixties. Their remaining tenure following my scheduleable retirement would be brief.

So, I began to privately explore options that could preserve continuing high value-added leadership indefinitely from Bill and John while inaugurating a new generation of young management fairly soon. I felt a compelling obligation to be a major influence on the establishment of the longer term leadership.

At all times and at that time, I was intimately involved and impressed with the special handful of potential chief officer candidates within the company. Over the autumn months of 1983 I mulled the merits of these able people. Each iteration clarified the adequacy of choices and confirmed the premise that we could confidently promote from within. Our management development program and environment had served this vital cause.

The more comfortable I became with those candidates and their degree of readiness, the more I leaned to finding a phased arrangement that would put in place "on my watch" the next generation of leadership of the corporation.

Bill Weisz and I were so close and had teamed so long I could almost think as he would think. Loyalty and objectivity were two of his superordinate qualities. He would have accepted the mantle of the senior office but was not consumed by the need to occupy it. Further, Bill had borne the aftermath of severe illnesses and openly paced his efforts wisely. On occasion he contemplated early retirement.

In early '84, I invited Bill to share with me (and shortly with John) the authorship of a plan for the next generation Chief Executive Office. His instant reaction was hospitable to the idea but naturally inquisitive. Within a day or two of occasional clarifying meetings, he bought in. His was the first demonstration of sheer selflessness!

We elected to let the matter rest and mature for a short while. The merit of the idea held. Together we agreed it now was right and proper that we invite John's reaction and participation.

John, a bit younger and more robust, could justifiably question a plan that did not allow Bill and/or him to occupy the top chair if only for a year or two. After all, many companies sequence their leadership frequently.

At first John was troubled. His deserving record and laudable ambition justified his initial concerns. The pros and cons of the fundamental idea were chewed over one-on-one, as well as together. By the second or third week John came to each of us and declared in his inimitable style, "Count me in." Selflessness again subliminally resonated through our executive suite.

Now the three of us were poised to think and work together to design the leadership plan for the long-term future. In time, during 1984, we brought two of our senior contemporaries and the Director of Human Resources into our confidence. For useful reasons we thoughtfully massaged the subject on into early 1985. With our unanimously "agreed to" plan clarified, I outlined our proposal in detail to the Board of Directors at the August meeting, 1985.

Our Board was cognizant always of its most important responsibility — the investiture of the right senior management. The timeliness of their essential involvement was most apparent to all in the mid-'80s.

Yet they were not prepared for the boldness of our plan. Over the years they had tasted and approved some unconventional assignments and titles which brought forth a mix of mostly agreeable responses wrapped around the enigma, "You often propose doing things differently, but at Motorola it seems to work."

No decisions were requested in August. The Board's deliberative attention was invited at least through the November and February meetings. Each member rose to the issue. All manner of confidential interactions were invited and engaged. All the right questions were raised and answered. Among them:

Do Bill and John really buy in?

Do we want the Bob Galvin change at exactly the early nominated time?

The youthful candidates are appealing. Are the particulars of their assignments, titles, maturities, etc., four square?

And so on.

The multifaceted deliberations surfaced valid detail variations and a couple of fundamental suggestions that enhanced the plan.

By February 1986, the Board embraced all the principles but deliberately reserved authorization. It did allow that we could bring the candidates into the know and into the process of finalizing the plan. Of course, we had to assure also that the expected enthusiasm for each one's individual role and the teaming of the eventual three would be for real. It was. What questions and concerns the candidates posed proved to be de minimis regarding the essentials of the Board's principles as well as the working prospective relationship among the nominees.

The plan itself is described in associate messages on following pages. The uniqueness of our ideas were:

1. *A clear and early proposal to the Board for its extended deliberation from mid-'85 to mid-'86.*

2. *The graceful leapfrogging from a vintage team of sixty year olds to a youthful Chief Executive Office team.*

3. *A clear, early announcement to all publics and first stage implementation of the Board's approved plan to allow an*

eighteen-month transition and training program for the new team from July 1986 to January 1988.

4. A special well-deserved recognition of Bill Weisz to carry the title of Chief Executive Officer during that transition period. An equally well-deserved recognition of John Mitchell to bear the title of Chief Operating Officer through that time though I would remain the highest authority officer through the transition and beyond. I simply retained the title of Chairman of the Board and we put the words in the bylaws and put the word out that this was the senior officership. The Board had a little trouble with the potential for misunderstanding as to the actual line of authority. A few people puzzled over the rhetoric but the recognition was right and it worked.

5. The addition of the third and even younger member who was nominated to the finalized three man CEO team which was to lead us into the early decades of the 21st century. He joined the plan in January 1988.

6. The retention of the service in later stages of the two selfless seniors, Bill and John, in the uncommon positions of Vice Chairman and Officer of the Board. They would remain full time, high prestige corporate officers. These positions were designated simultaneously with the installation of the new team members into their January 1988 positions.

7. The designation in the final stage of a continuing position of influence for me, Chairman of the Executive Committee of the Board, from which I support others.

8. The selection of the uniquely coincidental date of January 11, 1990, for the final act of the plan. That date was fifty

years to the hour that I performed my first company function as a banquet speaker at the 1940 Motorola Radio Distributor Convention. At that anniversary, I turned over the senior leadership to the able three — George Fisher, Gary Tooker and Chris Galvin, whose creative qualities will add multiple distinctions to the institution for another generation.

Announcement Memo
June 26, 1986

To: **All Motorolans**
From: **Bob Galvin**

This memorandum announces and describes a series of organization changes which over a period of years will put in place the next generation of senior management of the corporation.

One responsibility that the management and the Board have always considered paramount is seeing to the continuity of capable senior leadership. We have always strived to have proven backup candidates observably available, employed transition training programs to best prepare the prime candidates and been very open about a developed plan as we would approach the years of its implementation.

My father did this with me.

I did it with Elmer Wavering, a former Vice Chairman.

More recently in 1969 Elmer and I did it in moving the then youthful Bill Weisz to the corporate headquarters and Bill's ultimate transition to the Chief Operating Officer position in 1972. That organization change, for example, was publicly spelled out in 1969 and executed in steps, subsequently and successfully, according to plan. A somewhat less involved plan and announcement introduced John Mitchell into the Chief Executive Office in 1975.

Our experience and culture convinces us as to the merit of a planning, announcement and transition process that sets forth the steps over the full implementation period.

The prime objective of the plan announced today is to ultimately put in place key officials for the next generation of corporate leadership. We believe that one of the secrets of our company success has been generation-long leadership at the top. Paul Galvin headed the company for three decades. I have been in my position nearly as long. If a leader enjoys the health, zest and competence for the job, we believe that continuity is immensely valuable. When this is reinforced by the complementary continuity of the Elmer Waverings and Dan Nobles of an earlier era and the Bill Weiszes, John Mitchells and many others of recent years, we believe we have a distinctive leadership competence as well as a process to insure its continuing renewal.

The plan is phased in three stages, with a series of events that take place in one phase and may continue through another. Think of the stages as three parts of the future calendar.

Stage 1: *July 1, 1986, next week*

Stage 2: *July 1, 1986, to January 1, 1988*
(The eighteen month transition period)

Stage 3: *January 1, 1988, and beyond*

This memo will describe more than three events, but each of them will fit into one or more of the three stages in time.

Event A: The continuing role of the present members of the Chief Executive Office.

Bob Galvin: 63 (Chairman of the Board and Chief Executive Officer): As of July 1, 1986, I will relinquish the title of Chief Executive Officer. I will remain Chairman of the Board. That position is designated as the senior officership of the company. I will remain fully active throughout the transition period and beyond.

Bill Weisz: 59 (Vice Chairman of the Board and Chief Operating Officer): I am pleased to announce that the Board of Directors has unanimously and enthusiastically elected Bill to the position of Chief Executive Officer, a premier recognition of his superb and devoted service to Motorola for his entire business career. Bill will fulfill that position until January 1, 1988. Throughout that time and beyond he will continue in his other role as Vice Chairman of the Board.

John Mitchell: 58 (President and Assistant Chief Operating Officer): I am pleased to announce that the Board of Directors has unanimously and enthusiastically elected John to the position of Chief Operating Officer, a premier recognition of his outstanding and loyal service over his entire Motorola business career. John will fulfill that position and continue to carry the position of President until January 1, 1988. After that time John will assume the position of Vice Chairman of the Board like Bill Weisz.

The three of us will continue to work and lead the company full-time throughout the eighteen month transition period. We will bear our full responsibilities, execute to our full authorities, focus on our same areas of emphasis and cooperate in the energizing and directing of the institution just as before.

But we will additionally associate with, train and liberally participate in leadership sharing activities with the designees for later promotion to the Chief Executive and Operating Officerships.

Event B: The appointment of the next generation leadership.

On behalf of all of us in the present Chief Executive Office, I am pleased to announce the unanimous and enthusiastic election by the Board of Directors of George Fisher (45) to the position of Senior Executive Vice President and Deputy to the Chief Executive Office effective July 1, 1986. George is further designated to become President and Chief Executive Officer as of January 1, 1988.

On behalf of all of us in the present Chief Executive Office, I am pleased also to announce the unanimous and enthusiastic election by the Board of Directors of Gary Tooker (47) to the position of Senior Executive Vice President and Chief Operating Officer effective July 1, 1986. Gary is further designated to become Senior Executive Vice President and Chief Operating Officer as of January 1, 1988.

These two gentlemen, George Fisher and Gary Tooker, are proven managers and respected leaders with credentials well-known from their many years of service to the company. It is the intention of the Board that each will be elected to the Motorola Board of Directors in August of this year.

Event C: As of January 1, 1988, after the eighteen month transition period, the relationships of the five senior officers will be as follows:

During the early period, I will rank as the senior officer. For many years I have demonstrated a liberal willingness and ability to delegate out of respect for Bill and John especially, and many others as well. Thus, George and Gary, in that order, can step up and take charge of everything for which they can find the time. Further, they have concluded that they can work together, sharing many responsibilities and dividing areas of emphasis among them as have Bill, John and I.

Bill and John will obviously remain on the Board of Directors as Vice Chairmen of the Board. Each will be designated as an Officer of the Board. This is a new class of officership in the corporation, but not new to American industry. It is designated as a full-time executive responsibility in our company. The officers in these positions will fulfill multiple, major, timely assignments as directed by the Office of the Chief Executive or by the Board. Bill, John, George, Gary and I have come to recognize that there are a near limitless number of major issues and opportunities at the corporate level which, in recent years, have gone well beyond exhausting the value-adding capacity of our present three man office.

Motorola's management knows how to orchestrate this so that each of us can play an unfettered role while complementing and supporting the whole.

To any who may wonder if five people can relate in an orderly way, while vesting the required authority with the new leaders, we can assure that the culture is accepted and embedded by all. It has had our universal endorsement ever since Bill, John and I addressed this management transition process and the concept of the new structure. One great company, IBM, uses a somewhat similar structure very well. But even if no one else did this, we would do it because we have the need, culture, experience and dedication to participate well at this level, just as the company is doing in so many ways and places.

Announcement Memo
December 8, 1987

To: **All Motorolans**
From: **Bob Galvin**

In June 1986 I announced the plan of transition to the
next generation of Chief Executive Office leadership.
The transition has proceeded effectively and smoothly.
As anticipated, those changes will be instituted
January 1, 1988.

George Fisher and Gary Tooker have moved toward and
now into their full Chief Executive Office roles with confidence and competence. Their new era of corporate
leadership gives promise of grand achievements for many
years to come.

I am pleased to additionally announce that Chris
Galvin will move to Corporate headquarters as Senior Vice
President and Chief Corporate Staff Officer on January 1,
1988. He currently serves as Corporate Vice President and
General Manager of the high-performing Paging Division
in the Communications Sector.

(Additionally the memo reconfirmed the new positions
and roles of Bill Weisz, John Mitchell and others, as well as
the continuing senior role of Bob Galvin.)

Announcement Memo
January 12, 1990

To: **All Motorolans**
From: **Bob Galvin**

I am pleased to announce the inauguration of the next generation Chief Executive Office of the corporation. It is now fully constituted and installed, effective January 11, 1990, by unanimous and enthusiastic election of the Board of Directors. This ultimate expectation was substantially outlined to you publicly first in 1986. Each step to fulfillment has occurred smoothly as anticipated.

George Fisher (49) who has performed ably as President and Chief Executive Officer since January 1988, is elected Chairman of the Board and Chief Executive Officer of Motorola, Inc. This position is designated as the highest authority officership in the chief executive office and, therefore, of the company. George has served Motorola for 13 years.

Gary Tooker (50) who has performed ably as Senior Executive Vice President and Chief Operating Officer since January 1988, is elected President and Chief Operating Officer of Motorola, Inc. This position is designated as the second highest authority officership in the chief executive office, and therefore, of the company. Gary has served Motorola for 28 years.

Christopher Galvin (39) who has performed ably as Executive Vice President and Chief Corporate Staff Officer since January 1988, is elected Senior Executive Vice President and Assistant Chief Operating Officer of Motorola, Inc. and becomes a member of the Chief Executive Office. This position is designed as the third highest authority officership in that office, and therefore, of the company. Chris has served Motorola for 16 years.

I am also pleased to relate that I will continue as a full-time officer of the corporation in support of the new Chief Executive Office and all Motorola people. My new position will be Chairman of the Executive Committee — a newly constituted committee and position of the Board of Directors. I will retain no conventional line authorities. I will assume those authorities and assignments appointed by the Chief Executive Office and/or the Board as may be periodically directed. I will act daily as a corporate officer to advise and influence constructive ways and means in the best interest of the company.

We have a tradition of collegial and supportive relationships, as demonstrated by prior Chief Executive Office members serving in similar capacities. Bill Weisz and John Mitchell have served with the title Vice Chairman of the Board in support of our recent Chief Executive Office. Theirs is a quality-of-performance tradition I intend to emulate. John Mitchell will continue in his Vice Chairman officer role. Bill Weisz, recently retired, remains a non-officer Vice Chairman.

An additional personal word. I am 67 years old. I have served the company for 48 aggregate years since first having performed as a spokesman in the company on January 11,

1940, during student years. Yesterday, the 50th anniversary of that spokesman occasion, was chosen as the date of this appropriately timely change. I will continue to work with you and for you for some years to come.

Reaching Out to Leader People

Motorola was a fifty-million-dollar sales company shortly after World War II. The men running it were also about fifty. They were managing well.

I was being nudged along ever faster in my twenties. They, and even I, foresaw likely growth. It was evident that more leaders would be required. Yet the environment for other young folk to broaden and strengthen their authority and responsibility was not universally open.

The initial, established senior team justifiably felt a special sense of proprietorship and assumed it to be theirs for some years yet to come. It was "their" company. They held plans and facts to themselves (and to me) for the "good of the company."

I struggled with that. That wonderment made me particularly receptive to another's good idea. McCormick and Company—a spice and condiment purveyor—initiated and publicized a Junior Board of Directors. This Board of fifteen or so middle management people was encouraged to study most any corporate issue and recommend action to the senior Board. The personal development and corporate improvement prospects seemed self-evident.

I recommended we adopt their idea. Most of our dozen or so seniors were cool to the idea. It was deemed unnecessary. It would generate "make" work. When I indicated the Advisory Council to the Board of Directors (as we might call it) should have access to closely held data so as to fulfill its charter, the resistance hardened.

I wanted ever more and abler talent around. My father relented. We would ease into the use of confidential data.

The very naming of the first Council members spotlighted the actual quality of the next tier of managers which was being less than fully appreciated. Their early studies and suggestions were useful. Every one of the members went on to become influential officials, mostly because of their inherent skills and effective operation, of course. The Chicago-based Council was eventually cloned in Phoenix and together they continue to fulfill through each successive membership our highest expectations.

Councils of all kinds followed. Distributor councils. Function of business councils. Motorola Service Station council, the Science Advisory Board, etc. They became platforms for study, influence listening, advocacy, networking, personal development, et al. Participation abounded and abounds.

~

In time, my father placed me second in authority to him and announced we would act as one. Either of us could act on any issue. The other would support.

Many wondered how it would work. It did. We made it work.

Its titles over time: P.V.'s Office (Bob to be a part of it), The President's Office, The Office of the President. Years later, the Chief Executive Office.

The Office Of assumed significance, particularly to me. It was hardly an original idea here. Yet, the degree of potential application in the company that I vaguely foresaw then had an idea enhancement quality and potential that stimulated me.

If an Office Of at the top was to succeed, it needed candidates who had experienced and adapted to such a managing relationship role earlier in their career. It followed that the experience base had to be provided by similar assignments at business unit levels.

As many of the company's businesses enlarged, they too, would likely require the coverage of dual leadership. In fact, it seemed to me that such growth potential would more likely be achieved with the multiplier effect of dual leadership. As this need was being satisfied, the training and testing of the dual incumbents would become a valuable parallel benefit.

The Office Of has its disadvantages. Some incumbents just plain don't prefer it. "Leave me alone to run my own show" — or, "It's rough playing second fiddle." Mixed signals can emanate from the office. As a consequence, periodically some Office Ofs have not clicked. Some players departed or were benched.

But it has worked well more often. Throughout our continuing use of its structure and process we have advanced over our competitors. The proof is in the using. On balance, it is a figure of merit.

It has consistently provided frequent best informed succession answers. It absolutely helped to provide the proven source of Chief Executive Office candidates. Finally, in its special way it was another means of sharing leadership (participation) with more and better people.

~

In the '50s, I wondered why so many problems and questions were bucked up to the top people. The many men and women I knew in lab and office and factory seemed more than able to deal with most of them. I urged certain of our managers to work out some scheme to involve those closest to the subjects in problem solving and initiatives. The management efforts to do so were scattered and more often than not insufficient. The common wisdom of boss over worker was too entrenched.

Time. Too much time went by. Yet the issue would not go away. Walter Scott, who was at that time (circa 1960) heading our largest manufacturing operation, and I started an irregular series of late afternoon, unstructured meetings. He and others of his key people were searching for more promising modes of operation which led in those meetings to early seeds of a greater involvement of many more people.

There were others who were sensitive to the same needs. Each group learned from the other — even friendly rivalry played out among them. Early participative programs like BREAD (Better Results Earn Additional Dollars) were launched and learned from. Eventually, the fundamental principles of the company's Participative Management Program evolved.

~

The common thread, the uncommon thrust of these refinements of now ordinary ideas, is a reaching out to the leadership qualities that all people possess to a larger degree than traditionally appreciated.

Our appreciation of the existence and potential of these pervasive involvement/leader qualities came earlier than most. Their full potential is yet to be fully tapped. Of this I feel confident, our people at all levels of responsibility will rarely be found wanting as the appreciation of their qualities are more evidently invited and trusted.

~

My father urged us to reach out. The idea of reaching out to people — all the people — for their leadership contribution, yes, their creative leadership contribution is the most rewarding potential reach of all.

The *Total* of Customer Satisfaction

Our current progress on quality is exemplary. Together with shortening the cycle of time to do things right we are well on our way to six sigma operational performance.

A prerequisite to this accomplishment was the exploding of old conventional wisdom. Most of us used to take refuge in:

To err is human.

Excessive quality costs too much, takes too long.

Consistently beating our last year's numbers a bit was good enough.

Soft errors (like paperwork) were more excusable.

We're as good as our fellow Americans anyway.

Fire fighting our way out of a quality emergency in the nick of time was a badge of honor; it was even fun.

Today we can hardly believe we used to think that way. Because of enlightened wisdom that operating to zero defects is possible, is fastest, is lowest cost, is essential to survival, we can foresee that tomorrow our operations give promise to virtual perfection.

But will operational perfection by itself assure our superordinate goal of **Total** Customer Satisfaction? Not likely!

As leaders we have played a key role in these processes and achievements — learning why and how and seeing to the teaching of why and how to design for manufacture, six sigma, faultless order processing and on-time delivery from *our* catalog of products and services *we* elect to provide.

Senior Product/Operation leaders have other value-adding opportunities and obligations beyond the whys and hows. These include two key "what" and "when" factors. The what we elect to provide and the when we elect to provide from our catalog of products and services.

Our **customers want their entire or specific choice** of product and service **at their earliest** opportune **time.** If we fully satisfy that want of what and when along with operational perfection, we will achieve Total Customer Satisfaction. **If we provide the customer our choice** of product and service **at our time** plan along with operational perfection, we will only deserve credit for incomplete, less than total customer satisfaction.

Do we really intend **Total** Customer Satisfaction? Our traditional position has been:

We can't do everything.

We can only afford so many development projects.

Our share of Served Available Market (SAM) is good.

There are only so many good people.

There will always be projects on our cut-off list.

We've got to make a healthy profit first.

The conventional manager assumption has been, "My value-added is making choices. I'm the resource discriminator. Measure my finite choice of selections."

Sounds good!

So did yesterday's conventional wisdom!

The customer wasn't really satisfied then.

He won't be fully satisfied tomorrow either, unless we improve our what and when for every one of our established businesses and eventually our establishing businesses.

He won't be fully satisfied until we close the Total Available Market (TAM) gap.

And, what about our quest for the Total Imaginable Market (TIM)?

Each of our businesses has more competitors than ever. If a competitor discovers or anticipates (and many are) an alternate, a derivative, a unique application of our kind of technology to which we could or should have migrated earlier or a newly imaginable application of electronics that is "up our alley" or just simply elects to do the obvious that we postponed and **that competitor delivers**, then he satisfies our customer and we don't. Isn't it notable that:

He made a different decision.

He didn't cut and run.

He added value.

He found the people.

He found the money.

He'll make the profit.

That competitor may be playing a niche. But what do we suppose each of our offerings are?

That competitor may not be satisfying (yet) all of the "whats and whens" in our present (leadership) portfolio. But he just added one more.

That competitor has — and all of them together have — diminished and impaired our record of Total Customer Satisfaction and begun to raise his.

That should not be tolerated.

His (their) success should not be tolerated.

Conventional wisdom should not be tolerated.

We either believe in Total Customer Satisfaction or we don't.

In our defined or definable fields of interest — our Established and Establishing Businesses — we must accept and learn how we can:

Anticipate earliest every "what" that the customer wants when the customer wants it and/or any competitor can provide it;

Select every sellable, relevant project; resource promptly, effectively, uncompromisingly;

Maybe structure and staff differently; implement to the new time and sigma standards.

This challenge is no more heretical than the operations challenge of yesterday.

Its promise is no less rewarding.

It is a promise to be fulfilled "in the particular" — in each of the specific businesses by each of the specific technologies in which we engage.

Therefore, let us focus on key identifications and application of terms at this point to set the stage for eventually detailing our objective, concept and plan.

Motorola's chosen fields of interest are a broad range of electronic components, equipments, systems and services.

We will list the Industry Segments we chose to serve (Communications, Semiconductor, Cellular, etc.).

Within each we will identify the Established Businesses in which we are engaged (Mobile Radio, Paging, etc.; Power Transistors, Microprocessors, etc.; Base Stations, Subscriber Portables, etc.) and Establishing Businesses like Computers and new enterprise businesses.

The charts will reveal we are either established or are establishing ourselves in each product/market business.

Where established in a field, we are to adopt the attitude and standard that that field or business is our birthright. Having claimed that birthright, we are or intend to be deserving of an expectation level of that market's customers that we are the supplier of first choosing of all needs. We **will** fill all these needs!

If we are establishing ourselves in a field, we are to be guided by the same attitude and standard with the objective that that birthright is to be earned early by steady, rapid progress to full line offering.

The above two paragraphs flag the factor of time. In each of our Established Businesses we have a varying degree of blanketing coverage of the possible offerings accomplishable by any supplier. It is our intention eventually to blanket that coverage. All possible options will be identified and a roadmap of resourcing for the fulfillment of the uncovered options will be fully committed to promptly or shortly, in addition to the timely continuing leadership renewal of the existing products. The objective is that all these gaps will be closed by a certain early date.

In each of our Establishing Businesses we typically have a lesser degree of blanketing coverage of the possible offerings accomplishable by any supplier. It is our intention eventually to blanket that coverage. All possible options will be identified and a roadmap of resourcing for the fulfillment of the uncovered options will be periodically, fully committed to in addition to the timely, continuing leadership renewal of the existing products. It is the objective that all these gaps will be closed by a somewhat later date.

Steady, linear progress is to be made toward both goals starting from the date of adoption of this policy and program.

Each of these established and establishing business categories is classified "critical" because they are our birthright and thus our total satisfaction standards for operations and availability will automatically apply.

We will operate to these principles: once a real need of our prospective or current customer is identified as a defined, Selected Project to fulfill, it is obliged that the project be supported. The project will be fully committed to as a matter of policy. Resource allocators must presume and act full commitment.

If while preparing for and/or actually engaged in performing the full commitment, the resource allocators question the continuance of the full commitment, they can appeal through channels to the CEO for modification of the plan. The CEO may also initiate such question.

But note that the resourcing process is recast. The right to resources is automatic, presumed and obliged versus having to appeal for a grant. The authority to avoid, reduce or eliminate the resourcing is reserved to the CEO.

Whereas our culture, training and general competences will always aspire to a winning implementation of each project, thoughtful risk is to be encouraged and failure resulting from responsible efforts will be occasionally expected. As such they will be more than tolerated as having been worthy of the try and the likely peripheral benefits gained. Obviously, over time a level of confidence will be earned by the principal players. This will be a prime factor in the level of confidence vested under each resource leader in each "team."

Also obvious, we should expect best-in-class and successful implementation (yes, including best-in-class performance to full budget per project) on most projects.

Further, product/operation management is encouraged to advocate responsible added investment if unanticipated requirements arise. (No, we are not throwing money at projects. We expect managers to manage.)

One of the inputs that persuades us to this latter factor is the following:

McKinsey and Company has done a study that emphasized the importance of time to market. It employed a model of product life cycle, steady continuing price reductions and market growth much like many of our products. The conclusion of the study:

1. *If a new product introduction and shipment is delayed six months ($1/10$th of a presumed five year product life) the after tax profit for the life of the product is reduced one third!*

2. *On the other hand, if the first quality shipments are on time but the project has to bear a 50% development cost premium due to earlier engineering inefficiencies and overruns, the after tax profit effect was "only" 3.5%.*

Conclusion? We're for overruns? Of course not.

Real conclusion: Assuming quality design, time of introduction to market is a vitally important factor for:

1. *profit performance and*

2. *the Total of Customer Satisfaction.*

(Footnote to the above: Aren't product life cycles shortening? Won't the consequences of these factors compound?)

Thus, to restate our principles, no Selected Project will be purposely held back. All Selected Projects are to be resourced to accomplish best-in-class standard of completion and implementation. And all legitimate needs of customers in our critical fields of interest — our Established and Establishing Businesses — will require the assignment of a Selected Project.

The achievement of this overall plan is dependent on three other related factors among many.

First. *Increased foresight by senior professionals and managers — the premium will be on timely, accurate* anticipation *of technology potentials, engineering execution and customer needs and opportunities.*

Second. *The successful integration of and uncompromising performance to a superior, complete Technology Roadmap.*

Third. *Emphasis on and results of superior key human development and recruiting and facilitating to bring "the anticipated" to life.*

An essential tool in this process will be an Anticipations Registry. I envision that every idea for a new product or service will be listed at its source department and copied to a central registry office of the corporation. The format will begin with a ledger. Each line entry will be dated, along with the name of the conceiver/submitter, brief description and a limited edition of relevant essential facts. In time the data will be managed with a computer system that will permit all manner of collations.

The registry will be a record of Motorola's consideration of the idea, vis-a-vis when such an idea was conceived and/or acted on by competitors. The registry office thus will keep records of the initiation of ideas of our competitors as well as ourselves. Periodical evaluations will be made as to the record of our conceptions/commitments vs.

competitors. This process will allow us to grade ourselves on two important factors. One, our timely anticipations and commitments. Two, our failure to anticipate or untimeliness of anticipation and commitment. This evaluation will become a prime evaluation of leadership achievements of our principal people. Its greater value should be the universal stimulation of the "influentials" in the company to aggressively influence our destiny.

Our conventional first perception of this process will be the expansion of project budgets — added cost! This will be a valid, short term concern. We must early on transition through this.

The reciprocal, of course, is the reality of opportunities lost and/or long delayed. Both of these (opportunities lost and delayed) are factors in our current less than desirable profit performance. But more than that, they are major factors in our less than desirable satisfaction quotient of our customers.

There is no better time to move to the new mode of resourcing and product/business commitment than now. Most of our businesses are substantially in good stride. The cyclical phenomena we may face from time to time are not likely to be extreme. The arrival at the new standards of full, timely offerings will make us more resistant to later cycles and more achieving in every competitive environment.

The organization must persuade itself to embrace these fundamentals. All relevant managers will be involved in the refinement of the concepts and the fleshing out of key

elements of each appropriate part of a plan to institutional-
ize this management process and practice.

As we proceed to this goal we will explore and adopt
appropriate operational principles and procedures for
budgeting, measuring performance, decision making and
other practical factors.

Illustrative of these are: the Budget for each project is
to be realistically written to meet total customer satisfaction standards in contrast to a less demanding affordability
or convenience standard; performance is to be measured
on the quality of anticipation, quality of the product,
delivery to date, design within budget, design to target cost
and acceptance by customers.

Product/operation management is responsible for
selection of each project in concert with its senior management including Division, Group and/or Sector Officers.
Advocacy of a recommendation not to resource a project at
a compromise rate must be joined in by Division/Group
and/or Sector Officers (as assigned by the Group Sector
OGM) if it is to be submitted to CEO for consideration.

Failure to have anticipated an offering by competition
that competition successfully delivers or ignoring it will be
adjudged a serious oversight.

A key positive factor in the growth of and promotion
of managers is the leadership achieved by the responsible

product/operations official and their senior supporters in positioning our offerings so as to earn our customer's **total** quality and **availability** satisfaction.

Note: As this book goes to press in early 1991, the more outreach aspects of these ideas (*The Total of Customer Satisfaction*) are being reviewed at the senior level of the company leadership. No decision has been made regarding their entire adoption. A common and thoughtful reaction to the provision of automatic initial resourcing is the proper concern for affordability. The timing and staging of transitioning to it will be challenging. My instinct and faith is that it will prove doable. It will be reach out for sure, but with the utmost of creativity and perseverance, it can add to our ability to outreach our competitors.

PURPOSEFUL DIFFERENCES

"I don't mind a man who is dumb.
I can't stand a man who is numb."

PAUL GALVIN

Motorola Goes the Other Way

A pivotal idea grew on Motorola. It may have started as a coincidence or an instinct. But in the early years we came to recognize it as a way to go. Simply, but vaguely, put: whenever and wherever possible we tried to go the other way. Examples tell the story.

Paul Galvin was forced to find a new business the year following his founding. He went the way of mass producing a radio for a car. No one else was there.

When he could expand, he chose vacant land in a residential neighborhood on the west side of Chicago with no existent industrial neighbors. The land was a natural for manufacturing. Our job-creating presence was enthusiastically welcomed by the work-ethic residents. We had the area to ourselves for some years, relatively less noticed by unions and welcome by down-to-earth, upbeat people who appreciated the respect with which they were treated.

The special respect for people was itself a relatively uncommon characteristic in those days.

The sensing of the promise of commercial two-way radio was unique in 1940. Virtually no one else ventured forth. That field was mostly ours alone for years.

After the war the leaders of the company wanted a second center to attract technologists for the anticipated high tech future. Phoenix was chosen. At that time you could count on the fingers of one hand other producers there. Our folks figured right, the ambiance of the southwest would attract many postwar, outreach engineers if we could find the promising things to do. They helped us find them.

Later we tried to replicate the Phoenix success by offering to establish ourselves in Tucson, Arizona when it was still underdeveloped industrially. We would only locate in an area far removed from Hughes Aircraft. The community turned us down.

As we were prospecting for laboratory/factory sites in Europe, we explored the conventional large city industrial districts, among others. When the economic development agencies advocated their preference that investors locate elsewhere for better geographic balance — a betterment for their country — we saw promise of mutual benefit. We became pioneer employers in Toulouse, France and East Kilbride, Scotland. Both were "new" towns.

One last site story. Schaumburg wasn't yet Schaumburg, at least as we have come to know it. It was all farms and stables in the late-'50s and early-'60s. We salted away three hundred acres then as a place to which we would likely need to go. That fortuitous land acquisition was facilitated by an earlier, smaller acquisition in an unconventional but attractive Chicago north side area that was never used by us. The appreciation in value of the smaller site coincidentally afforded the new location of what was to be the future corporate headquarters, the Communications Sector Headquarters and the company training center on the now sprawling Schaumburg, Illinois campus.

But physical facilities are only the most picturable pursuit of going our way. The expansive appointment of officers, early discovery of the participative people principles well before adoption by so many, embracing an uncompromising quality standard before most other American companies, our obliging that suppliers commit to compete for the Malcolm Baldrige National Quality Award, an act of faith that a mammoth training effort was essential and would pay, and the installing of an Intelligence Department which has yet to be copied are examples of the operational ways we employ unconventionally.

The venture into semiconductors was our most radical redirection as a previously equipment only manufacturer. Few electronic companies dared such a move and most of them did not succeed. The conventional wisdom even within the company was "don't risk it" or at most, "invest only to make for internal use." The minority-held view was that the economics of size required broad line merchant market choice and this propelled us into a new business orbit.

Paradoxically, staying put, at times, is in fact a further manifestation of going a unique way. As noted above, we successfully established the company in the transistor business. Then the industry evolved to integrated circuits.

Most of our competitors gravitated primarily or exclusively to ICs. We, too, moved effectively to ICs but saw the continuing essentiality and growth in transistor devices as well. Both courses were steered rewardingly.

Cellular radio telephones and Japan are two of the more noticed unique subjects regarding directions of the company as this essay is composed.

Only AT&T, along with ourselves, had the vision and determination to seek and proceed into an unchartered mobile telephone market with a cellular concept. No other American enterprises would enter or stay the course through the '60s, '70s and '80s. The Japanese and Europeans entered late but well.

The overall Japanese electronics challenge makes for a perilous business adventure unto itself. That Motorola story is told elsewhere. Reference to it here merely notes that Motorola, mostly alone, ventured "where angels feared to tread" and found its way.

The Idea of Ethics

At an early point in history the Christian-Judaic Ethic was resolved from creative ideas. Once its essential principles were conceived, it (Ethics) and they (its Principles) were no longer a subject for further creativity.

The title of this essay is The Idea of Ethics. The inclusion of such a title in this book that espouses more and more creativity is an antithesis. Here at Motorola, the "idea" of Ethics is the rejection of creativity — the avoidance of some clever justification to do wrong.

The company has its Codes and its Principles. They are soundly based on the Ethics cited above. And they sound like the other fine standards of many other high-principled American-founded companies. These are basicly rooted in and communicated through the Golden Rule and the civil rules of the Ten Commandments.

Most often our application of them is a simple black or white, wrong or right determination when we have the facts. Because we set aside the economic factors, we do not allow a gain to be won or a loss to be suffered to taint our ethics class of decisions.

Ethics decisions are readily reached. Some may have unwelcome, subjective consequences which cause the temporary wringing of hands, but objectively, they are most straightforwardly concluded.

One major experience of long ago continues to model the essence of our stance.

A youthful contemporary came to my office one day in about 1950. Our conversation went substantially as follows:

"As you know, Bob," he reported, "we have been negotiating to the conclusion of the large Microwave Radio Relay System for a South American country. I'm pleased to report the customer has accepted our system proposal and is ready to conclude a contract. However, a new and unacceptable condition has been prescribed that you must know about. You won't like it. We don't like it. Be assured we full well understand that we cannot accept it.

The original range of the price negotiations has been ten million dollars. The new wrinkle is the suggestion that we revise our bid up to eleven million dollars as if further services are going to be performed or guaranteed. That one million dollar increment will be meted out by the local agent/distributor 'as required.' What is all too apparent is that key officials there will pocket it.

We have been informed this is traditional and pre-sumed to be proper in that region. We have been advised to adapt to the native way. Don't worry, we will not. But you must know of this unacceptable twist. Of course, you may have a suggestion as to how to deal with the problem."

He and I clearly understood the favorable financial consequence of this additional Microwave billing. Our annual corporate sales had not yet approached two hundred million dollars and our annual profit margin after tax ranged around four percent. Using those two round numbers as a base, the South American order would have boosted our sales over five percent — a significant rise — and our net profits would have surged by some twenty to twenty-five percent because all of the company's overhead and indirect costs had been absorbed by the balance of the year's other business. To fail to accept this order meant a significant impact on all the profit sharing employees in the company and a notable earnings and evaluation differential per the stockholders' shares.

One could ponder what was right for each of them, particularly if some other American competitor was to take the order and financially profit by it. There was no need to ponder. To us, there is one overriding determinate. It is improper to profit from an illicit act.

I responded to my associate, "Thank you for the objective report. My compliments to you and all the involved officials in the division for the forthright and high principled application of our code of conduct regarding payoffs. You ask if I have any suggestions. Yes, I do. First, I join with and applaud your refusal to compromise our principles. Second, let's have it understood, in case others have not yet considered it, that we will not take the order even at the original price were it now offered to us. Third, let's have it further understood that we will take no other new systems orders from that administration of government in that country."

These additives were a surprise to him. In fact, to his knowledge, the sales people had already started some strategizing directed to putting the deal back on the right price track.

"Your reaction goes farther than we anticipated," he said. "Is that necessary? If so, why?"

I replied, "Remember, your instincts and judgments were right. On these we agree. What additionally have we learned? The officials of that administration are on the take. Others who do business with that administration know they are on the take because that is how and why those suppliers obtained their orders. Some others, like us, know they are on the take from their aborted efforts to do business honorably. It follows that all of those supplier companies and officials, and those they confide in, will assume we make payoffs if they learn we received a large order from that administration. Our integrity would be impugned! You, our associate, (including profit sharers and stockholders) and I could not stand for that."

That example, that message echoed through the relevant corridors of that and other businesses in the company. Even for a grand and apparent financial gain, we would not compromise.

The title of this essay might better have been: Ethics, **The** Idea. Everything else good depends on it. Without integrity, character, et al., our other ideas could not sustain.

APPLIED MATERIALS

From: DENNIS HUNTER

The Intelligence Department

Early in the Nixon Administration, I was appointed to the President's Foreign Intelligence Advisory Board. This Board had been established by President Eisenhower in the '50s to take cognizance of Soviet compliance with treaties and agreements and to directly report to the President the Committee's views as to the adequacy of U.S. general intelligence competence.

The Board was composed of approximately 10 people mostly with extensive public service backgrounds — other than myself. I was known to have devoted study to the issue of national security affairs. As a consequence of this and other credentials, I was tendered the appointment. The important aspect of this experience as it relates to the ongoing governance of Motorola was that I came to have a fundamental appreciation of an intelligence process and department.

The common view of an intelligence operation is that of a spy-directed, clandestine information collection process. Even heroic acts come to mind. What I came to realize was that the more important continuing value of an intelligence department is the gathering of fact and information from all manner of common, open sources. The data is employed and enhanced by the processes of analysis and evaluation. Estimates of competitor activity and purpose can be drawn. Options for response can be proposed. The nature and quality of the product of this work can be (and has proven to be) of special significant value beyond the other useful market research functions we also employ.

Circa 1970 our company was engaged in a substantial review of our competence as a strategic thinking institution. We concluded a healthy spirit of discontent. We were incidentally doing good strategic thinking in places within the Corporation. But our process and output were inconsistent. We engaged experts, in-house studies, refined definitions of terms, and set out to train ourselves to upgrade our strategic thinking.

I learned from my President's Foreign Intelligence Advisory Board experience that one of the tools of inestimable value was the intelligence department that could augment the intellectual qualities of our broad cast of thinkers — strategically and otherwise.

I concluded that the idea of establishment of a true intelligence department was essential. I persuaded our relevant key officials. They were willing to initiate, experiment with and hopefully permanently support the continuance of a professionally driven intelligence department.

This would take a special quality of leader. After extensive search we found a distinguished official of the Central Intelligence Agency who saw the promise of the application of intelligence principles to industry. This idea had not been tried seriously in American industry. Regarding Japanese practice, we were not so sure. We hired this capable official and gradually built a modest size organization to demonstrate the utility of this unique function.

It goes without saying that the department was established with the clear direction that it would never engage in illicit, covert action, or accumulate information in any improper way. We were convinced that there would be more than sufficient public information from which we could interpret trends, directions and understandings of a highly useful nature. By applying the processes learned from agencies, we would end up with determinative information to shape strategies.

Few companies have adopted this idea. We now recognize it as a distinctive competence which with greater frequency provides our thinkers with better insights, analysis, estimates and options. These enhance our ability to both respond to immediate business conditions and to lead our institution to a more promising future.

The Technology Roadmap

I've always visited labs. In the '60s I prowled them. It was
fun. It was the best way to learn by osmosis some of the
engineering so well known by many of our best people.

Not being an engineer had its limitations. It also made
for an advantage. I began to discover critical voids and
thought of an idea to close them and open other prospects.
I discovered projects unknown to or unappreciated by
operating senior management, product potentials essential
to our strategies that had been turned down or improperly
resourced and bright people with so much more to offer.
In spite of this, remarkable invention and development was
also pouring forth. We were just self-satisfied with less
than optimum results.

On the day of one of my visitations my discontent
about the voids boiled over. As luck would have it,
the other top corporate people were in session with that
business's general management. I joined them as was
expected but unloaded my dissatisfaction which was not

anticipated. "The quality of our technology governance was deplorable in this and major sections of our company!"

In that meeting I declared the need for some kind of a roadmap that all of us were to drive. The term stuck. Then and there a technology roadmap was directed to become a permanent program in every business. We sketched out various charts and forms to visualize time vs. specification, vs. available technology, vs. expected or potential technology, vs. market need, vs. competitive comparison, etc.

Six principles were prescribed within days:

1. *Dual commitment by division general management and the CEO office to everything on the roadmap was to be obliged so that the division could not unilaterally rearrange its resources vitiating a strategy counted on by Corporate, and Corporate could not by fiat change a budget or allocation without complete consultation with the hands-on business managers;*

2. *Twice a year full agenda reviews would be prioritized, scheduled and conducted with Corporate;*

3. *All factors and data were to be documented — to be tracked on paper;*

4. *Roadmap reviews and reports would have a minority report to assure that the initial or current non-supported projects received a further hearing or were not forgotten for later support;*

5. *The Technology Roadmap Program was to be put to work "now;" and*

6. *The plan could be improved as we learned better to use it.*

It was not that we did not have product planning at the time. Our product company had obviously grown through two score years. In fact, there was excellent anticipation of need and planning in places, but even each of these missed using a key planning feature of one of the other Divisions. One would use product life cycles vitally. Another would dabble. Some derived future product insights from learning curves. Others ignored that technique. Most of our top line managers were engineers. Good ones. Some of them took their apparent natural grasp of the whole of technology potential too much for granted.

Paradoxically, we needed the discipline of attention and system to free-up the ready ideas of our many fine engineers who hungered for true and timely support. Those of their ideas which were sidetracked, when recovered and put to work, would earn so much more customer support and higher profit. Regrettably, some of us in leadership had been too caught up in managing costs vs. employing a system that could create more opportunities.

The Technology Roadmap Program is now a vital tool but is not yet perfect. Altogether it organizes

1.   *the fundamental description of the particular business, including its product, its product life cycles and learning curves;*
2.   *detailed, sophisticated technology and projected needs and forecasts;*
3.   *"quality" requirements and the technology and processes to achieve;*
4.   *matrixes that relate competitive comparisons;*
5.   *resource allocation estimates and commitments of people, equipment and facilities;*

6. *patent plans and potential; and*
7. *the Minority Report.*

The Roadmap now has a leveraging impact on virtually everything we do operational. Its historical value is not just that it solved our earlier problem of dropping designs between the cracks. More than that, it has built for us new sets of tracks with brighter, high tech lights at ends of well defined product and technology open-ended tunnels.

The Welcome Heresies of Quality

The story of Motorola's effort to improve Quality is portrayed in many ways. In this brief essay I focus only on beliefs about Quality. In fact, challenges to old beliefs.

As we found ourselves being challenged or challenging ourselves regarding the merit of an established belief regarding Quality, we realized that, literally, we had to turn over a new leaf most times that we needed to achieve a major advance. One at a time we were obliged to make an heretical act of faith change.

Eventually, a new revelation about a certain historic guideline or standard added into a basket of heresies.

A heresy is a challenge to a previously unquestioned 'truth.'

The singular idea that finally clarified was that there was a common thread and relevance to the valid challenging of many old testaments. We could combine an integrated aggregate of useful, believable, welcome heresies.

Here, simply in litany format, are:

The Welcome Heresies of Quality

OT Quality control is an ordinary company and department responsibility

NT Quality improvement is not just an institutional assignment, it is a daily personal priority obligation

OT Training is overhead and costly

NT Training does not cost

OT New quality programs have high up-front costs

NT No up-front cost to quality "quality programs"

OT Better quality costs more

NT You cannot raise cost by raising quality

OT Keep measurement data to a minimum

NT You cannot have too much relevant data

OT To err is human

NT Perfection is *the* standard — *total* customer satisfaction

OT Quality improvements come only from small continuous steps

NT Partially true. But radical step-function improvements are essential and doable

OT It takes extra time to do things right

NT Quality doesn't take time, it saves it

OT Haste makes waste

NT (Thoughtful) speed makes quality

OT Quality programs best fit products and manufacturing

**NT Quality's most crying needs and promises are
in services**

OT Thou shalt not steal

**NT Thou shalt steal (non-proprietary) ideas
shamelessly**

OT We take care of our company — our suppliers better
beat the price

**NT An essential to being a world-class quality
company is to be a world-class customer**

OT Old Testament

NT New Truths

Challenge any or all of them if you will. Each challenges us
to be better than otherwise we would be.

THE CUSTOMER IDEA

"Never forget your old friends."
PAUL GALVIN

What is a Customer Visit?
An Idea Breeds an Idea!

In the mid-'80s, as our quality improvement program accelerated, someone put a bee in my bonnet. The idea? Get out and really listen to customers.

At the rate of better than one per month through most of the first year, all day meetings were scheduled for me with customers of each of our generic markets. The purpose was investigative. My process was highly personal; often the solo Motorola visitor. The involved customer personnel were those dealing directly with our product or service. If possible, I tried not to take the time of a customer's official unless that official felt his or her message was vital to emphasizing a suggestion or complaint.

Each day's agenda flowed variously from designer, specifier, buyer, receiver, assembler, inspector, quality supervisor, installer, repairman, warranty manager, payable clerk, marketing specialist, etc. Anyone whose job at the customer was made easier or harder as a result of the quality or insufficient quality of our product, system, service or paperwork was invited to lay all facts on the line. Each did.

Each trip report ran ten-to-twelve typewritten pages. Each reported item was followed up by incident and for permanent change.

Prior to each visit, full briefings were presented to me by the division and its sales representatives. After the first four or five customer calls two basic patterns were evident. Essentially the same mix and intensity of compliments and complaints would be emphasized from all customers. And our sales people knew and mostly had reported on every factor I heard from the customer's personnel.

As a result of living out this idea we learned:

1. *We could be doing substantially more business with each customer if in their words we would only "clean up our act."*

2. *All officers and some special employee teams adopted similar customer visit responsibilities (some officials, of course, had a consistent history of such involvement).*

3. *The real meaning of, and visceral feeling for, total customer satisfaction was indelibly instilled in most of us* **for the first time!**

There was another revelation. It spawned another idea. Empower our sales people! Fully!

Every complaint I reported, every suggestion I made or referred on was dutifully dealt with by each organization. The same was true of the response to the reports of the other key managers' trips.

Why did we fail to be fully responsive to the same, earlier plea from the sales rep? Why were sales representatives being too selective now about their reporting legitimate complaints? Because of the earlier unheeded pleas?

The self-evident idea! Empower the sales representative with virtually the same power and influence of the CEO. Turn the organization chart right side up. Put the customer on top. Let experienced sales people listen, heed and then convey and insist on timely action in behalf of their customer. Trust the experienced sales people! Act! What a powerful idea.

Heretical, too. The rest of us thought (or maybe still think) we knew better. But each new customer visit reinforces the balanced understanding of and responsible advocacies of our experienced sales people almost all the time. Consistently betting on and acting on their day-to-day customer evaluations would improve our averages up to six sigma customer performance. Their insights on future requirements are also remarkably helpful in sorting out tomorrow's opportunities simply because they speak for their customer.

Some trials of greater empowerment now are being employed. A bit of progress has occurred. Even where tried, many sales people are timid about "taking charge." That tells us something also.

If, and I prefer to say when, this organizational idea, this organizational culture is universally embraced, our customers, finally, will have the best possibility of achieving total satisfaction.

Our Idea Behind Training

In 1979 the officers of the company had committed to improve our Corporate quality in large measure. Shortly thereafter I came to vividly recognize what should be so obvious. Improving the company should mean personal improvement by each of us individually.

About the same time, the issue of companies being more competitive again took on a special focus. It seems that every five to eight years the issue of competitiveness reasserts itself throughout the business community. We then intensify our questions: What techniques improve quality? What savings improve competitiveness? The spectrum of particular employable ideas is vast.

I kept searching for a common denominator. Where could we put our resources that would leverage most anything and everybody? The search for that answer led to the earlier instinct. Individual, person by person, improvement.

Once that concept was reenforced I sharpened the questions: "How do I improve my quality to where I am as good or better than Mr. Kobyashi, the distinguished head of Nippon Electric?" "How does our Vice President perform as well or better than the Vice President of Texas Instruments (pairing each of our people with his or her counterpart)?"

As I searched for the answers to those questions, I realized I didn't know what I didn't know. I needed others to advise, to consult, to help me to be better on apparent as well as yet unidentified subjects.

It took only the smallest step to the conclusion that what I needed personally, what our vice president was going to need, what each of our people were going to need, was a thorough program of education, tailored to our special vocational needs. The assignment: a revolution in our training program!

The Company had training for decades. At times we had superb training for particular cadres, such as the Executive Training Institute in Vail and Oracle, Arizona decades earlier. But the prior and existing programs were grossly insufficient. So we closed down virtually everything for a fresh review.

With appropriate personal preparation, I went to my direct associates and asserted: "In order to achieve our quality and competitive objectives, we are going to launch a superior and personalized training program." The principle was readily agreed to by all, but conditionally. The concomitant reaction was that we must do it in a way to consume little time and even less cost. Keep overhead low. That, typically, is the proper reaction of disciplined managers. But in this instance it could not be the determinative factor. I was obliged to see the idea from a more promising point of view and stand for it. I insisted: "I don't know how you are going to account for the flow of cash that will have to churn through the training program, but I am convinced that training will not cost us net money at any time." I had faith that almost the instant we would train the right subject that those trained would achieve savings. I went out on a limb and avowed that even though it was clear that we were going to have to employ from $30 million to $50 million a year within two years after we'd start, it would net improve the cost of doing business. The counterpart gains forthcoming from training itself would more than compensate.

The apparent cost troubled most officers through the early phase, but they acquiesced to my uncompromising confidence. As expected, early success began the turn to an enthusiastic, eventually universal, support and use.

By the mid- to late-'80s, training, superbly designed and executed by its staff and guided by a distinguished insider "Board of Trustees," came to have the greatest single impact on the quality and competitive performance of the Corporation. Every Corporate activity was elevated. All-encompassing training became an indispensable person-by-person tool for total customer satisfaction.

Motorola Suppliers "Opt" for the Baldrige Award

The company had won the Malcolm Baldrige National Quality Award in the U.S. in 1988. The healthy reaction within the company was characterized by the prideful expression, "Great, but now we'll really have to work all the harder to prove that we deserve it."

The company's quality effort was wrapped up in its title, Six Sigma, and its reach-out goal of virtual perfection by 1992 — the 3.4 defects-per-million standard which statistically defined the title. We were adjudged worthy of the award because the actual quality of our company operations was very high, excellent processes and policies for achieving such standards were producing consistent predictable results and, incidentally, showed genuine promise of accomplishing steady improvement.

The healthy spirit of discontent harbored in the realization that we had to work even harder and that we were yet obliged to achieve the far-out six sigma goal set many of us to reexamine what else we may need to do.

Within weeks our Corporate Quality Office decided to set the next challenge — to recompete for the award in the mid-'90s, as soon as we would be eligible again. An exciting string of improved practices, processes, training tools, etc., perked from many quarters of the company about that time also.

I admiringly reflected on this insatiable appetite for ever better "do differentlies" that our associates were brewing. Certain of them catered importantly to our suppliers. This emphasis naturally flowed from the various cooperative efforts with suppliers that were step-by-faltering-step nurturing a partnership relationship with more and more of our vendors. A notable part of this effort involved many of us making more frequent and penetrating supplier visits to learn from them how better to relate to them. I made my share of such visits and reports.

So there was a real and proper focus on the significant role of our fine suppliers. As I mixed and matched the myriad of factors regarding the suppliers' impact on our quality objectives, I joined with others in the realization that a consistent attainment of six sigma quality could only be earned if our suppliers were aspiring to essentially the same ultimate performance as ours, except much faster and more purposefully than the then current trend.

How to move all of us forward? That became the operative question. As I cast about for ideas to contribute, the existence of the award and the motivation of the supplier fraternity converged. Go for the Baldrige! Prepare to go for the Baldrige!

I presented the idea to our top quality pros. They knew our suppliers. They knew the award criteria. They appreciated that suppliers' attention to the award's higher standard criteria would be a winning combination for all of us.

They, the pros, and my CEO associates and our procurement officials instantly bought in.

The plan as I presented it would oblige each supplier of minimum size to commit to us in writing by mid-1989 that their company would eventually compete for the award and begin early to prepare seriously for that eventuality. Such a commitment maintained the supplier's qualified position with us. Those unwilling to file such a commitment would be disqualified as vendors at year's end.

We were sensitive to a range of reactions but we concluded that the idea and plan were right for the supplier, right for our industry and right for us.

A good number of suppliers saw the benefits. Many others were puzzled and even troubled. Scores were incensed. Some of those forfeited our account and expressed themselves accordingly.

Almost all complied with a declared intention to go for the award and within a year most were applauding the assignment that was beginning to significantly enlighten, upgrade and hasten the suppliers' quality standard and cost standard of performance.

To the extent that we have suppliers different than a competitor, ultimately we will have a possible advantage. To the extent that many electronic manufacturers procure from the same higher quality supplier, we'll all be better off. If all of us serve customers better, a healthier industry base will emerge. In the long run this will be in our mutual best interest.

This act of leadership bothered a few. It was controversial at the outset. What little heat we were obliged to take from suppliers then increasingly warms the hearts of our more satisfied customers now. Our customers, of course, are the vendor's customers as well. As the last of our suppliers come to fully appreciate the essentiality of higher expectations and the potential for virtual perfection, the merit to them of the Baldrige option will be even more accepted.

But the idea does not end there. In fact, it cannot have a fulfilling ending unless we seriously embrace a complementary bright idea of others in our company: we, Motorola, must become a World-Class Customer.

On Being a World-Class Customer

Motorola is the customer of its vendors. Of course, it is a
prime responsibility of the vendor to strive to totally satisfy
us. Our customers hold us to uncompromising standards.
They and we must require the same from our suppliers.
Our standards are embodied in the company's Six Sigma
quality principles. Performance to those standards by our
suppliers is required.

It is also obliged that we, the professional procurer
of their parts and services that interplay in our products and
services, must provide the most encouraging environment
and practical basis for the suppliers' optimum support
and performance.

Our suppliers account for about one-half of our input
and output. Thus they are accountable for about half of
our quality performance and costs. If there are policies and
practices of ours that inhibit suppliers from doing their
best for us, we shortchange ourselves.

There is a valued slogan, "The Customer Knows Best."

It is well for a company like Motorola when acting as the seller to be guided by that principle.

But when an integrator company like Motorola is the customer of its many specialty suppliers, it is essential to acknowledge that often our vendors know best.

Our expert engineers, specifiers, facilitators, system establishers, buyers, etc., must have determinative roles in the procurement process. But we in Motorola are not all-knowing in each specialty.

Experienced, credentialed suppliers must be listened to more and their advice more often followed at the earliest possible stages of our interrelationship with each other. The industry-wide, long-heralded but insufficiently embraced principle of value driven, consistent and long-term, mutual benefit partnership relationships must not escape us.

With greater frequency than we have yet been able to admit and practice, suppliers could be helping us more on tool design, base materials specifications, standardization, definition of even higher standards, clever features, improved systems, etc. Suppliers could, if we would better let them.

Letting them more, encouraging them more, recognizing and acting to this need more will move us to becoming a truly world-class customer. As a world-class customer we can better assure our place as *the* world-class supplier in our chartered markets.

Being the world-class customer in our industry is an idea whose time has come.

GLOBAL STRATEGIES

"Reach out, do not fear mistakes."

Paul Galvin

Three Uncommon Linking Strategies

Most studies of strategic thinking are silent on what ought to be a first or early principle. The principle of writing the rules.

To have the most effective influence on writing the rules, a second principle for rule writers is to have a strategy to ingratiate themselves to the system.

Thirdly, to demonstrate the application of the first two strategic principles, it is useful to focus on another factor insufficiently emphasized in strategic thinking — the principle of sanctuary.

When I was a youngster in the business, circa 1940, I was intrigued with the fact that the leaders who were founding our fledgling two-way radio business were frequently taking the train to Washington, engaging in discussions with those who made regulations like the Federal Communications Commission. They were setting up the standards, the radio frequency spectrum and the rules of the road for that business. They were determining how a two-way radio system could be used best by varied users throughout our country.

This struck me as a generic process whose results could have leverage impact on many affairs of the company. So I watched and studied their efforts with great attention. Of course their efforts were always guided by and aimed at having the most legitimate and universally effective rules with which all participants could equally engage. But because my senior associates were employing the power of authorship, the initial thinking that was going into the developments of these rules challenged them to be doing the most advanced and complete thinking as to how we could effectively employ these in the best interest of our customers.

While I was in high school, I took courses that taught that in America we the citizens were the sovereign power. We could write to our congressman; we could conceivably influence the passage of a law or the establishment of a regulation. The work of the leaders of our two-way radio business was demonstrating the application of this principle in its most tangible way.

I was the boss's son. I was working to ultimately merit some role of leadership, and it was clear that I had a favorable opportunity to rise to a position of influence in the company. And so I took note of the fact that if writing rules was important and helping to write rules was allowable, then I should prepare myself to be one that could have effective influence on writing rules, whatever they may be.

Without having a clear plan ingrained in my mind, I early on had scattered thoughts about how I should go about earning my credentials and ingratiating myself to the system as one who might someday be listened to.

In today's vernacular I launched a personal strategy of building relationships, networking with those of influence in our society, without knowing exactly what each future step would be, but being in motion to learn how to earn those credentials. I no longer remember all of the detailed activities that were the roadmap of this strategy. They started with such simple things as networking better within the company, even to and including doing the best I could on the company's sports teams. I reached out within my neighborhood and tried to help an occasional senior member of the neighborhood on local issues. There are so many civic and charitable organizations that need the help of volunteers. I would respond affirmatively occasionally to an invitation to help. Or, I would reach out to another organization, when I felt that it was deserving of some service.

Early on I noticed that some of the major leaders in the city were identifying with their political party of choice. I was invited on fund-raising teams and to assist in a few of the ceremonial political events. And then more.

My father had endorsed activities in the trade association. He told me many times of the values that he was gaining by his interrelationship with his customers, his suppliers and his competitors in the association. So when it was timely I took my place in their activities. With increasing confidence I made more suggestions and soon I was named chairman of committees.

Eventually, all of these identities began to reinforce each other. Subsequently, I became the president of the Electronic Industry Association. I chaired the largest political dinner in Chicago for a President of the United States. I was asked to testify before committees of the Congress. I had taken a serious interest in public issues such as national security. And each one of these and the responsibility displayed became a base for additional invitations like membership on the President's Commission on International Trade and Investment, the House Committee on Administrative Review, which was an ethics study for the House of Representatives, the Industry Policy Advisory Committee to the Special Trade Representative (I became its chairman during the Tokyo round of the Multilateral Trade Negotiations) and the President's Foreign Intelligence Advisory Board.

Throughout these phased experiences, occasionally the proposition would be raised by others — should I enter government? Should I seek elective office? That was an easy decision. I knew that this would not be pleasurable and effective from my standpoint. But what I did sense was that I could play an ever increasing influential role if I were to act from the various public advisory roles.

What rules would we want to write? I've already referred to writing rules that enhanced the two-way radio business. But there are rules in virtually every phase of business. Taxes, antitrust, defense, and many more, including international trade. International trade and the problems associated therewith, became a prime area where the writing of the rules was going to be of major importance to our Corporation.

By 1960, we had become a substantial enough company in the United States that we were acting more purposefully to expand to Europe and Asia. We made forays into each market over the course of the next few years. Early on we had relatively receptive experiences in Europe and the Middle East. There were certain rules and regulations there where we played varying degrees of influential roles.

When we went to Asia we discovered that the circumstances were often different, particularly in Japan. The Asians were interested in selling to us, but we found less receptivity in their buying or receiving us as investors. Without knowing the essential words then to describe our instincts, it was our feel that we must ultimately penetrate the Japanese market and others in order to achieve the economics of a size that would make us productive and competitive. We understood that it would be to our disadvantage if competitors who thrived within their home market were not challenged by us in their home market.

Later on, this feeling was synthesized for us by scholars at the University of Michigan who verbalized this instinct — the principle of sanctuary.

A sanctuary is readily picturable. In military terms one does not wish to let one's enemy have a sanctuary across a border where he can rest and rearm, and then come back and do mischief in our field of battle. The principle is the same in business. If competitors have a sanctuary in their home market they can continually strengthen themselves, then come over into our markets skillfully, and/or do mischief before they have investment here at risk.

All in all we knew that we had to have an influence on writing the rules that prevented competitors from having a sanctuary. Or, put in the affirmative, we required open access to discipline competitors if necessary in home markets while earning timely share of market.

This is a classical demonstration of the interrelationship of strategic principles. The ultimate principle of the three was the prevention of competitors having sanctuaries. The enabling strategy principle was applying the means of writing the rules of trade, both with the American government and having an influence on the Japanese government. The personal strategy of preparing to possess credentials to influence the writing of the rules was an idea adopted early without knowing just how it would be applied, but ultimately being ready if opportunities attained.

One of the incidental but consequential results of this personal investment in public affairs was the interpretation by the Japanese of the multiple contacts and influence that Motorola had. I had worked moderately in campaigns and knew presidents casually, but it became apparent that I was well-acquainted with a large number of their principal appointees.

Chuck Percy, one of my very closest friends, had been in the United States Senate for 12 years. When the Republicans assumed the majority upon the ascendency of Ronald Reagan as President, Chuck Percy became the Chairman of the Senate Foreign Relations Committee, another Motorola contact in the eyes of the Japanese. And so it went...from Nixon days and people, Bob Strauss and other Carter aides, etc.

Because each of us is prone to evaluate the other's situation based on our own experiences, the Japanese businessmen who have a major interrelationship with their government and substantial influence there presumed that the same opportunities existed for people in my position to especially influence affairs in our government. Indeed, our government officials did listen to businessmen of all persuasions. Fortunately in many instances our points of view were appropriate and prevailed, and our government gave us support, thus assisting in gradually opening the Japanese market.

Meeting the Japanese Challenge

In measuring up to Motorola's obligation to meet the Japanese challenge, the uncommon ideas were sought and uncovered to make way for operational people to do their remarkable job of successfully investing and selling in Japan. The follow-on from the ideas also aided others in the company who were to be responsive to Japanese predatory practices in the United States market.

One standard mode of managing is to select and assign key goals among officers. In the late-'70s, the Chief Executive Office and other leaders of the company composed and refocused on the then "Top Ten Goals." One of those was Japan. The issues associated with that goal were initially assigned to me. It was a broad assignment dealing with anything and everything necessary to open the market in Japan for investment and sales and the defending of the American market from Japanese practices here, such as dumping. Bill Weisz eventually was assigned this area of emphasis.

Early on we recognized that one factor that would determine our success was organization structure. We were already globally oriented. We had assigned all non-U.S. market responsibility to each cognizant U.S. division head-quarter. For Japan, we were obliged to question that conventional structure. We were going to require focused energies in order to deal with the uncommon problems vis-a-vis that country.

A few of us deliberated on this issue frequently. Often, I would open my blackboard to capture, to illustrate, to relate fledgling ideas.

We consciously and subliminally used various creativity techniques. The better we pictured our business as a system and the supporting factors, the more readily the idea emerged that for Japan we must assign one senior, experienced, universally accepted operating leader to devote full time as Deputy of the Chief Executive Office with authority for all business and relationships in Japan and all relationships vis-a-vis Japan in the U.S. We simply gave him the name — Mr. Japan.

To control and lead this diverse product and geographic responsibility, we came to realize the need for one top boss in Japan. We simply called that person — Mr. There.

The defending of the American market yielded the same conclusion — a single lead authority here with (you guessed it) the name — Mr. Here. The apparent simplicity and obviousness of this plan was far from self-evident initially. The creative process was strained frequently. It was nursed by a mood of survival and the good fun of playing with picturesque names.

The structure change was contrary to tradition and past success. But the merits of the idea, apparent to the creators, did not take extraordinary persuasion with the division heads. They, too, appreciated the serious challenge and uncommon problem. They were willing to give and take.

The final structure preserved a substantial direct interrelationship between the divisional headquarters and those active and domiciled in Japan. Because of the superb leadership quality and acceptance of Mr. Japan, Steve Levy, the organization structure was launched with the least disharmonies and became uniquely effective.

The second idea was, as with so many ideas, an unexpected derivative of separate and different pursuits.

Pursuit number one: the operating people of the company were doing an ever-improving job of sharpening the quality of our designs, products and services. We were winning a high majority of the competitive contests with the Japanese in non-Japan markets.

The second pursuit: the company became more oriented to advertising to the public vs. just the trade. Institutional advertising nevertheless is debatable. We were experimenting with one or another effort but still puzzled about a continuing campaign.

The third pursuit: just reacting to our publics. In the '70s, a universally prominent public and private question from friends and professionals was, "How are you doing against the Japanese?" We were able to say that the Japanese competitive efforts were a real challenge, even a threat, but that mostly we were winning in the U.S. and Europe under normal competitive circumstances. The reaction from those who would hear these private conversations was enthusiastic pride and renewed faith in America.

On one of those days we were in conference with our advertising agency considering valid and appealing, but conventional institutional ad themes. In the course of our ringing hands over them, I raised the question, "Is it possible that we may have an idea from within that may have appeal?" I went back over our many conversation experiences wondering if it would be possible for us to design a series of ads that would ask and answer the question, "How is Motorola doing standing up to the Japanese challenge?" Could we point this to targeted influentials like government officials, engineers who specified our products, purchasing agents and officers of private and professional organizations?

As I rambled on, the reaction of my senior associates was uniquely positive, almost more so than my own. With sufficient support we turned to assignments — testing the composability of yet-to-be-selected subject matter. We were obliged to conclude that we officers were the only ready ones already reciting "the story." We (which turned out to be me) had to take a crack at authoring at least the essence of the first ads.

I went home over the weekend and wrote the first three ads on a pad of paper on my knee. Those three ads are noted as an appendix to this chapter. Others that I wrote, and that the agency wrote over the next couple of years, attracted just the audience important to us. For the years that they ran, they persuaded many readers that American companies like Motorola were meeting the Japanese challenge and deserved encouragement.

The ads did attract attention to the corporation. But the most valuable service they performed for us was to establish a receptivity in the minds of private sector and government influentials. When Motorola asked that trade and investment rules be appropriately applied or modified, officials knew we had been working and investing responsibly and our cause likely had merit.

Elsewhere in this book we speak to the importance of the idea creator and advocate having credentials to influence writing the rules. This ad campaign turned out to be a key to creating the atmosphere and credentials so that influential people willingly listened to our appeals.

Introduction to Japan Ad Campaign

As the 1980s opened, Japanese business successes seemed to be undermining Americans' self-confidence.

Motorola saw U.S. companies, including Motorola, competing successfully against Japanese firms. It saw a future in which Japan would open up its domestic market, previously closed to many U.S. goods, or suffer serious trade consequences.

That vision became the basis for "Meeting Japan's Challenge," a series of advertisements reaching opinion leaders in business and government.

The campaign was a success, as measured by audience research, and its contribution to subtle changes in Americans' attitudes toward the critical issue of U.S. industrial competitiveness in a new age of global competition.

The complete series of advertisements numbering twenty-two, appeared in leading U.S. business magazines and newspapers between August 1981 and September 1985. Here are the texts of the first three.

~

Meeting Japan's Challenge
First in a Series

Is Japan's Challenge to American Industry Going Unanswered?

"What are you doing about Japan?" It's a question we are asked almost daily.

It may be the single most important question American business faces. The challenge to the U.S. economic position that Japan poses is serious.

Starting now and for months to come, we're going to be answering that question — in public.

Obviously, this is a subject on which many companies can speak out and should. We are doing so because we believe it will be good for our country, good for Japan, and good for Motorola.

It will be good for America to correct the impression many Americans have that Japanese businesses are in some way inherently superior. That impression is false.

It will be good for Japan because Japan relies on a strong confident America as a trading partner and ally.

It will be good for us because by learning how Motorola is meeting the challenge, you will have a more balanced, accurate view of our ability to serve our customers best anywhere in the world.

Now, don't get us wrong. We respect Japanese businesses. They are our customers and suppliers, as well as our competitors. And they are very good.

But we also know there are many things American companies like Motorola do extraordinarily well today. And we have an exciting commitment to do things even better in the weeks and months to come.

At Motorola, these things take the specific form of the development of new technology, employee participation in management, quality standards, accomplishments in productivity, effective cooperation with our government in foreign trade, and many other programs, products and plans of a company that is succeeding now and committed to perfection.

These will be the subjects of ads to come.

Motorola understands the challenge from Japan.

You can be sure we're not leaving it unanswered.

~

Meeting Japan's Challenge
Second in a Series

Could the Individual Hold the Key to an Entire Company's Productivity?

Many factors contribute to productivity; producible designs, superior tools, clever processes, minimal regulations.

But, heading the list is people. Most of us are aware of the impressive productivity improvements Japanese companies have realized with their people by using teams of cooperating workers called Quality Circles.

Wisely, hundreds of American companies now are duplicating these efforts in their factories.

At Motorola, over a decade ago, we initiated a plan of our own. Today we call it the Participative Management Program (PMP), and it reaches beyond the factory floor. We believe it has helped us achieve the same, and often better, quality and productivity results for which Japanese companies get credit.

PMP is an effective way to get the individual worker more involved, responsible, informed, and therefore, more productive.

Any individual worker can suggest things about any job he or she does that a supervisor may not know as well. As management listens and acts, quality and output rise.

In PMP, teams of employees meet frequently, sometimes daily, among themselves and with support groups to tackle the basics. Everyone is encouraged to define problems and suggest solutions. The management listens, contributes, acts. Each team operates to high, published standards which it participates in setting. The teams measure their improving performance to these standards daily, weekly, monthly. And everyone benefits.

Employees who want to can communicate additionally by submitting written recommendations. These are posted on prominent bulletin boards and must be answered in 72 hours. Not just with words, but with changes in tools, procedures or policies when humanly possible.

The results have been dramatic. Quality, output, and customer service are way up. Costs are down. Our jobs are more satisfying.

One-third of our 45,000 U.S. employees are operating under PMP today. Building on our years of experience, the balance of our U.S. operations will be fully managed through employee participation in 1983.

If we are succeeding well now, and we are, imagine how much better we will be soon.

There is much more to PMP that we'll be talking about in ads to come. You see, we believe what we've learned about productivity and the American worker can help other companies as well.

~

Meeting Japan's Challenge
Third in a Series

**How the Simplest Business Principle of All
Turns Competitors into Customers.**

If you make a better quality product than your competition, customers will buy it.

We at Motorola have seen this simple principle make significant differences in the international electronics industry we are part of.

For example, in recent years quality improvements by many Japanese companies have resulted in major inroads for their products into world markets, especially in consumer electronics.

But the same principle of quality has turned some of those Japanese competitors into important customers of American firms such as Motorola.

A case in point concerns communications equipment Motorola designed and built for NASA. Our equipment has been used on every manned and most unmanned space shots without a single mission-endangering failure. Not one. So impressed was the Japanese Space Agency with the quality of our space communications technology and our reliable performance they have specified Motorola equipment for use on many of their space missions.

Closer to earth, a Japanese national named Junko Tabei, the first woman ever to climb Mt. Everest, used an FM portable two-way radio made by Motorola here in America

to help guide her to the top. It withstood nights of 20°
below zero and days of blinding blizzards. Small surprise
that with plenty of Japanese radios to choose from, Ms.
Tabei also specified Motorola for her next climb, this time
to the roof of Tibet.

And the examples go on. Even though Motorola has
bowed out of the consumer electronics market, Japanese
companies that are today's giants in that industry buy
millions of quality components from our Motorola Semiconductor Products Sector.

All this isn't happenstance. It is the systematic result
of Motorola programs, pioneered and developed over the
past decade, to give all Motorola employees a greater sense
of involvement in, and responsibility for, the quality of the
products they design and manufacture.

So, when we receive quality supplier awards from
companies such as General Motors, Control Data and even
Hitachi, we know why.

And we're proud of that kind of response. It supports
our belief that quality is not only the oldest and simplest
principle of business. It also is the most important.

Industry-to-Industry Trade Negotiations

A high tech working group session was convened at the U.S. — Japan Business Council meeting in 1982. Saito-san, the head of Nippon Steel at the time, chaired the session.

He set the stage in my favorite way. "Does anyone have a fresh idea — a new approach to address our trade imbalance? At these and other meetings we too often gravitate to bashing and other unproductive pursuits."

I automatically put the creative process in gear, privately surveying factors and questions familiar to the problem and quickly related within my mind a range of processes and involvees. Various combinations sorted out until moments later one stood out: we, the participants in the meeting, had never convened a specific industry-to-industry pow-wow for a consequence such as our chairman challenged.

I raised my hand. Saito-san seemed a bit reluctant to call on me early. Was I going to repeat my often aggressive advocacies on increased access to market?

Shortly, he did recognize me. Whereupon I posed the following thought, "Is it possible that the answer is mostly in our own hands? So often we pose issues involving business overall or solutions dependent primarily on our governments. Why not sector specific industry-to-industry negotiation on trade or investment or disputes? Can representatives of the Japanese electronics industry meet and negotiate with representatives of the U.S. electronics industry? Each of our buyers and sellers and investing parties have it within our respective power to effect a noticeable part of solutions. Why not?"

Well, there were many why nots. Antitrust! Who could represent who? And a dozen others. But Akio Morita of Sony and I warmed up to the idea after a long afternoon walk. The plenary conference added the subject to its agenda. It was received coolly but not rejected out of hand.

The bottom line? Morita-san and I each recruited four of our peers from each country's electronics industry and convened a two day meeting in Honolulu months later. An American attorney observed. In that meeting we discussed and negotiated a written, signed agreement in principle for the American industry to better serve and the Japanese OEM buyers to purposely increase their purchases of American electronics goods. No preferences to the participants in our conference was countenanced. We presumed to deal in the best interests of all our peers in industry.

One of the minor turning points of our discussion was my appeal to the Japanese (in the American vernacular) to wear two hats: their corporate self interest; their country's broader interests. At our farewell celebration dinner I presented each participant from Japan with two Greek merchant sailor hats of different colors in appreciation of their broadminded objectivity.

The conclusions were publicized and reported to our governments. Some constructive activity initiated and a moderate number of companies from each country contributed or accomplished some modest buy/sell results. The effect faded but the merit of the process itself was not lost.

In late 1985, a major dispute over semiconductors brewed ever hotter. Morita-san called me from Japan and expressed grave concern in behalf of his country and solicited my counsel. At some point, one or the other of us recalled our industry-to-industry meeting. We concluded it was worth testing the process again if we could recruit appropriate representatives. In this case we hoped to add not only the lawyer observer but a member from each government. Four key U.S. semiconductor leaders agreed to join our company's top semiconductor executive and me. Akio was equally successful in enlisting senior leadership from five major broad line, electronics companies in Japan. Also, the Japanese government saw merit and allowability to appoint a major MITI official, Tanihashi-san, to join and, in a way, to colead that team. Our government could not see its way to be represented but were fully informed regarding the event and intentions.

Two serious issues loomed. Access by U.S. semiconductor suppliers to Japan's OEM market and alleged dumping of memory circuits by Japanese producers into the U.S. market. Industry representatives could not talk price (dumping). On the other hand, access in behalf of all suppliers was an allowable subject for discussion with the users. On May 15, 1986, we convened in California and concluded successfully an agreement in principle for a major step function increase in market share for American company-supplied semiconductors into Japan. Each delegation reported these results to appropriate government officials which led to the access section of the 1986 "Semiconductor Agreement." Although Japanese and U.S. officials later disagreed as to the true meaning of particular provisions of that section of the agreement (the 20% market share goal by 1991), some incremental business results were forthcoming.

Without the sector specific industry-to-industry negotiations there may not have been any Semiconductor Agreement. Opinions vary as to the merits of the overall agreement. But the fact is that the basis for step-by-step market opening continues to derive from this experience.

What is the promise of future sector specific industry-to-industry negotiation? It could be favorable. It's an idea whose time may come.

**Report and Mutual Agreement of the
Follow-Up Meeting to the Third Small Group
of the 20th Japan-U.S. Businessmen's Conference**
(Electronic Industries Trade and Investment Relations)

November 3-4, 1983
Hawaii, U.S.A.

**Action Program for Expansion of Mutual Trade
and Investment Between the U.S. and Japanese
Electronics Industries**

As a follow-up to the discussions of the Third Small
Group of 20th Japan-U.S. Businessmen's Conference in
Chicago in July 1983, some leading executives of the U.S.
and Japanese electronics industries met in Hawaii on
November 3 and 4, 1983 to discuss various ways to expand
amicable economic relations between the two countries.

The discussions covered a wide range of subjects,
including the economic conditions in the two countries,
bilateral trade imbalance and exchange rate situation. In
particular, the members recognized the need to improve
the current trade imbalance.

Obviously, consideration of bilateral imbalances must
not be limited to the trade account, and the trade imbalance must be discussed in a multilateral context, as well as
a bilateral context. Also, government efforts are indispensi-
ble for improving the bilateral trade imbalance between
the U.S. and Japan.

However, present circumstances call for active efforts

on the part of U.S. and Japanese companies to improve the bilateral trade imbalance as we expand bilateral trade.

During the discussions, the participants agreed that for more balanced trade, both country's electronics industries must make special efforts to create a climate wherein supplier and customer will have a reasonable sense of confidence to invest all appropriate resources to serve and be served in a promising long-term sourcing relationship.

The participants took note of the perceptions in both countries that:

U.S suppliers have, in notable instances, inadequately served Japanese customers, which has tended to discourage sourcing from the U.S.; and

Access of the Japanese electronics market has not always been as available or encouraged as it is intended to be now and in the future. This has tended to discourage a number of potential U.S. suppliers from making the commitment needed to earn a sourcing relationship.

The participants agreed that:

Both country's electronics industries have many companies with substantially equivalent competencies, resources and standards of performance;

Long-term relationships must satisfy the ongoing commercial and competitive needs of quality, value, delivery and service;

The participants should return to their respective companies, industries and governments and implement and seriously propose to activate specific programs. Such specific programs include, but are not limited to, the following:

I Japanese Efforts to Expand Electronics Imports

A. Further efforts to be exerted by individual electronics companies. Each company should recognize the necessity of increased importation of U.S. products as a corporate policy, and make efforts to take effective measures for this purpose, for example:

1. *Place higher corporate priority on increased imports from the U.S.*

2. *Encourage the establishment of more long-term sourcing arrangements with U.S. firms on a competitive basis.*

3. *Make all its employees fully aware of these necessities.*

4. *Whenever the occasion arises, have senior management write or speak in public to promote the importation of U.S. products.*

5. *As necessary, consider sending corporate buying missions.*

B. Further efforts to be exerted by the electronics industries as a whole:

1. *There are already government organizations, such as the Japan External Trade Organization (JETRO), the Manufactured Imports Promotion Organization (MIPRO), and private sector organizations, such as the Electronics Industry Association of Japan (EIAJ), that are already available to facilitate imports into Japan. The industry should encourage these organizations to educate the U.S. electronics industry to ensure full use of their facilities while expanding their services in*

behalf of the increased import objective.

2. *Promote the use of JETRO as an information center to facilitate efforts by U.S. industries, particularly small enterprises, to export to Japan.*

II U.S. Efforts to Expand Electronics Exports to Japan

A.   In response to the above efforts of the Japanese side, American electronics companies should exert greater efforts to export to Japan. The following are especially important:

1. *Establish higher corporate priority for securing their earned share of the Japanese market, with appropriate resource commitment to meet the special needs of the market.*

2. *Commit to long-term serving of the Japanese market to the full standard of performance expected as to quality, price, delivery and service.*

3. *Increase high-level management involvement in serving the Japanese market, including travel to Japan.*

4. *Send corporate selling missions to Japan.*

B.   Further efforts to be conducted by the electronics industry as a whole:

1. *Encourage U.S. Government efforts to stimulate other U.S. firms to pursue opportunities in Japan.*

2. *Participate in efforts to establish an information center in Japan to assist all U.S. electronic firms.*

3. *Encourage the development of a number of Americans knowledgeable of Japanese culture, business methods,*

and language and who have the necessary business skills so that American companies can more effectively communicate with Japanese customers and partners.

III Efforts by Both the U.S. and Japan to Expand Trade

In order to expand world trade and to enhance free trade:

1. *Both industries should support further efforts to open markets by reducing tariffs and other barriers to trade and investments through bilateral arrangements and multi-lateral arrangements such as the Tokyo Round.*

2. *Private companies in both countries should expeditiously respond to the requirements for quality, cost, delivery and after-sales service in each of their markets.*

3. *Measures for technical exchange and other business cooperation should be promoted on a commercial basis to establish a stable, long-term and friendly relationship between U.S. and Japanese companies. Foreign direct investment is desirable in each other's country. Efforts should be encouraged to eliminate legal and tax impediments, both national and local, to direct investment and to reduce social, political and cultural resistance to such investment.*

4. *In view of the increasing high technology developments of the electronics industries, proprietary rights recognized under the laws of each country in technology and software and their use should be duly respected on a mutually fair and reciprocal basis. Efforts should be made to avoid the*

possibility of abuse of such rights, which abuse may be an impediment to widespread use of the developing hardware and software technology and the expanded trade and investment it can generate.

5. *In view of the increased diversification of the electronics market and growing sophistication of products, efforts should be made to introduce consistency among various standards in different countries. Study should be made and action taken as to how foreign industry interests can be better represented in the process of formulation, revision and implementation of such standards in each respective country.*

6. *Specific problems in the electronics industry should not be addressed through abuse of the legal system, or allowed to become so politicized as to adversely affect friendly political, diplomatic and social relations between the two countries.*

The Prospect of Dominance
of the Service Industry

In the mid-1980s my intense attention to the international trade and investment issues that affected our company led me to search out a better and broader understanding of the consequences as a whole on our country. As I "hunted up" the facts of the relevant events and prospects vis-a-vis Japan's various activities and competences, a fundamental idea struck me. As I related and recast the bits and pieces of the trade/investment activities a new envisioning emerged. I would put the thesis in essay (and eventually speech) format. Then, and for a few years thereafter, virtually everywhere I asserted it, it was acknowledged as an unexpected and concerning possibility. Here is the 1987 composition of the idea:

We are increasingly invited to discover the power of information. I wonder if we are ready to recognize the immensity of it, and the eventual consequence of it on the republic.

It is the new power of information to manage certain key business sectors in the interest of the nation's economic leadership that excites me.

Let me put that promise in historical context.

The major changes in the life of man in recent centuries were driven by the Renaissance and the Industrial Revolution. These and related developments made for the establishment of economic empires: the Dutch, the Portuguese, the British. Thus, in part, history was made on a grand scale.

Are we now in the process of living out an historical epic of similar scale? It is likely! And it is likely that it may be very different than the conventional wisdom would conjure with major impact on us.

Much has been written to extol the potential of the information age. We seem wrapped up in bringing that age of age. As exciting as are the miscellaneous and aggregate achievements of thousands of entrepreneurial spectacular events and institutional successes, I foresee a grander vision.

I foresee an opportunity and a likelihood that the nation which masters the grand management of information for the prime services industries of the service sector along with ownership of key parts of the service sector in the major developed world markets is destined to global economic leadership of historic proportions. The consequence on the information processing and information communications industry in that leader country will be dramatically favorable. The consequence of being home based in an also-ran country will be comparatively debilitating.

This vision or theory can best be pictured and justified by postulating a scenario. A good case can be made that the United States will assume this role. We are strong in services today. But I believe I can capture the home audience attention more readily by making a case for another country.

I'm going to postulate as to how it could develop by Japan. In describing my version of a Japan vision and opportunity, I present it with profound respect and admiration for Japan and its people. I respect and admire their many qualities and for this topic, particularly, their ability as a nation to envision, strategize and execute a total plan. I will treat this thesis entirely in that positive tone.

I present this vision in their name as they are in my judgment in a better position at this starting time to ultimately fulfill the possibility. I present it as a competitive possibility, if not likelihood, in hopes of awakening and broadening the most fundamental strategic thinking of the business and political leadership of the information age centers of Asia, Europe and North America. I present it in eight short steps.

First, note singling out the service sector as the determinative arena. The prime services include, at least, hotels, investment companies, banks, insurance, hospital chains, communication carriers, transportation, construction, trading and merchandising. The identification of the service sector as the key marketplace subject to economic leadership is not borne of the conventional proposition of doomsayers who proclaim the hollowing of manufacturing corporations and the attendant consequence of a nation drifting defensively but safely into a service economy. Rather, I identify the service sector as the prime focus because it will naturally ascend in greater than previously anticipated importance everywhere in the developed world alongside of a viable industrial base. I identify the service sector because it naturally is the largest sector of all advanced economies by a factor of at least two-to-one over manufacturing. I also call attention to it because there is no God-given right that the established parts of the service sector of a nation are indigenously reserved to the native. For those who have thoughtlessly assumed that service businesses are immune to international reconstitution there needs to be an awakening to the new reality.

Second, I anticipate that 25 to 50 years from now the home economy of Japan will be predominantly service sector driven — more than its present 60% share of the whole. Japan's stewardship of manufacturing will be but little deemphasized. Yet its production will be more dispersed throughout the globe and substantially directed by services from home. Japan's real thrust will have moved more into the prime service business arena.

Why? Because it's the most natural and promising thing to do. It is said that Japan has few natural material resources so it must acquire elsewhere, add value and export. Ah, but it has the finest natural resources of all — its people, collectively.

Of course there are superb people elsewhere, everywhere in the world! But certain unique, coincidental and
earned qualities suggest the emergence there of a collective
distinctive competence at managing services with information. Their homogeneity; their culture of consensus; their
instinctive will to rally to this vision; their constantly
improving education system layered on their universal high
literacy can focus the next generation or two into a knowl-
edge-worker society. Such a society can project superior
aggregate skills to generate and manage information software, equipment and systems along with the resultant
information itself to an unparalleled scale. Think of the
consequence of additional millions of knowledge workers
marshalled to this cause.

After all, who hasn't wished for their children a move
up the professional ladder away from the toil of the soil,
or the factory bench, to the white collar environment with
a greater claim for the brain. I suggest that all advanced
societies tend to this goal and some will move to it more
purposefully than others.

Third, the Japanese have acquired, and will continue
to enlarge the wealth to invest in prime service sector
businesses at home and abroad. Theirs is a high-rate-of-
growth foreign investment program already. Even today
that program has heavily emphasized service businesses.
Investment banks and hotels are well noted. Japan's
ascendance in general banking is spectacular. Insurance,
retailing, distribution, medical services, etc., can naturally
follow. Zaitech — a Japanese term for financial technology,
earning on investments in others' businesses — stimulates

the appetite. Currency ratios favorable for property purchases and increasing opportunities to convert debts owed by others into equity ease the affordability of such investments.

What people own, they manage. What they own and manage also directs their sourcing policy. In fact, it is axiomatic that one's foreign investments create a market for one's parent company exports, which of course will include the electronic equipment and software to process and communicate their service sector information needs. And from this volume base will evolve additional values appealing to third-party purchasers.

Fourth, the Japanese must export to survive. It follows that in the new era they will export services on a larger scale. Yes, and they will be welcome. Where have you had better service than in a fine Japanese hotel or department store? The spirit to serve is there.

Fifth, it takes more than spirit to serve and control the information needs of any parent company's worldwide service chain. It takes what our profession has to offer — the ability to manage data and communicate information and knowledge wherever and whenever.

Let us inject here, parenthetically, another strong word for America. The American information age profession takes second position to no other at this time.

Yet I must return to our scenario with a **sixth** factor. Who can practice for this future main event any better than the Japanese? In addition to potentially marshalling millions more soft-technology and hard-technology practitioners, designers, and managers, the Keiretsus stand available as the systems test bed or beta site to various new standards, architectures, protocols, systems, products, networks, including patented designs and copyrights. The Keiretsu — a giant group of related companies — can see the virtual service sector literally under one roof. It's a bank, a trading company, a factory, etc., all wrapped in one. Each Keiretsu is an in-house market worthy of its own information and service sector investments — a microcosm of the prime services world, the likes of which there is no other. There are many wealthy Keiretsus, each able to exploit this grand scale opportunity.

Seventh, the structural revolution in the telecommunication carrier industry further opens the door for the type of radical change that I hypothesize. When each country had its primary (virtually single) telephone system, it was an anchor to stability, even inertia. Although national policy in most places limits ownership to natives now, watch carefully. Bypass, value-added, private networks, and the like will seed more change. The world has never known a competitive condition such as may be on the make in the carrier business of tomorrow. At the outset of such change we are prone to see mostly the promises of the new way. But the diversity of carriers and alternates will generate its problems as well as promises. Excesses are bound to occur. Rescues will be required. Consequences such as those represent opportunities to others jockeying for major positions in the service sector/information age scenario envisioned.

Eighth, some critical and possibly proprietary developments of leverage proportions are likely to be discovered in these next few decades. They may be determinative as to which center of the world will clearly take the lead. Will it be the stretching of the use of artificial intelligence? Will someone achieve a practical, affordable, automatic language translation system to render the global management of information systems truly users friendly? Recall that earlier reference to invention and copyright? The Japanese propensity to patent and increasing capacity for creativity cannot be dismissed. Their influence to establish new standards to serve services is not beyond the realm of reason.

Will the inherent nature of a country's national structure prove a strength or a weakness? Will America's required occupation with defense and its obliged large incremental allocation of thinker resources to this less commercially productive purpose give way to those countries that concentrate on civilian business objectives built on a "consumer market" mentality as in Japan? Will a nation's potential for success be affected by its encouragements or restraints of intercorporate cooperation?

Well, that's the scenario.

The service sector will be key to future economic leadership.

Japan is headed to service sector emphasis.

It will invest worldwide in services.

And it will so export and transact internationally.

The Japanese can practice this on a systems basis better than any.

While changes at the carrier level and/or proprietary developments can have determinative effects.

Our profession provides the key means for a nation's worldwide service sector success which in turn will affect our success.

The result, a likely opportunity for one nation's investors/managers to achieve a disproportionate — possibly overwhelming — role in the world's service sector economy of the early 21st century. There will be concomitant higher degrees of opportunities to that nation's information processing and communications suppliers.

As we arrive at the conclusion of this presentation, initial reactions will begin to form. They will span a full range. The general proposition deserves to be questioned, of course. The eight component parts I have identified will play out differently in detail for sure. But I respectfully suggest that the developed world will move in this direction.

More than suggest, of the following I am certain: this class of thinking is going on in Japan right now. You can be sure that capable, permanent research institutes there are engaged by assignment in this breadth and depth of strategic thinking.

They know there is a shapeable future out there. They believe they can reach it optimally by willing it rather than wishing for it. And so should we.

When my father was preparing me 50 years ago to assume the leadership of our little radio company, we could prepare for the future by merely anticipating each opportune derivation of a current offering to the next development, applying it in a separate virgin market.

But microprocessors and supercomputers and satellites and all the rest have shrunk time and distance and imposed on us the need to cope with structurable markets of global proportions. The strategies to win these will require national dedication.

It won't come easy but Americans must come to the reality that to retain the leading world economy we must plan for it — together as Americans. We must get about the ways to do it now.

Yes, I call for national goal setting in our interest and hold no fear that this will inhibit you or me to enterprise freely. My friends in Japan have long admonished me for our reluctance to collectively think ahead while saying, "How can you blame us for our success, when we plan for it?"

The way America does it will be decisive, for sure. I will urge that this strategic planning process aimed at optimizing American leadership in key businesses, including ours, in global markets:

1. *Be shaped primarily by businessmen's guidance which will*
2. *Be formally allowed for and supported by the federal government to assure world access,*
3. *Federally financed, partially,*
4. *Commissioning the finest thinkers from all walks of life. And,*
5. *Using the logic tools of our profession to synthesize certain complex issues.*

Among the harder hurdles we will have to surmount is to allocate time to such a purpose soon. We are naturally preoccupied with exploiting the power of our profession to the opportunities of the day. But we will be time and survival foolish if we do not initiate soon.

I for one have been around long enough to know the satisfactions of achievement borne of long and ready anticipation and the disappointments from failures to prepare early. Up to now these successes or failures have been enjoyed or suffered at the individual private enterprise level and averaged out.

But in the immediate century ahead the effects will aggregate. The primacy or the mediocrity of a collection of critical service businesses and manufacturing industries like ours integrated globally will determine the incremental economic strength of the country. And that economic strength is the foundation of the republic.

And so the three conclusions are:

1. *A nation's information industry helps make possible the global scale and dominance of the world's prime service businesses.*

2. *The American information industry will be either beneficiary or also-ran in that new environment depending on the American will to succeed with the whole.*

3. *The prosperity of our prime service businesses and the electronics industry are central to the affordability of the republic.*

That is the power of information.

Note: As of publication of this book, the fundamentals of this thesis and its associated recommendations have not taken root. Time will tell if ever they contribute some influence.

Renewal Revisited

Sprinkled throughout these essays are references to acts of renewal. Renewal is the driving thrust of this company. Literally the day after my father founded the company to produce B Battery Eliminators in 1928, he had to commence the search for a replacement product because the Eliminator was predictably obsolete by 1930. He never stopped renewing. Nor have we.

In one's twilight years associates ask the elder to review the past and project the future. My reflection is simple but poignant. I have witnessed 50 years of surprises to which few then existent competitors adapted. One might wonder if 50 years from now — the year 2040 — many of our current competitors will be a factor.

Speaking in the vernacular of our industry, I account

for 16 (bits of) surprises that have shaped the electronics industry from 1940 to 1990.

Radar

Magnetic recording

Television

Semiconductors

Employability of the extremely high radio frequencies

Satellite communications

Cellular telephone

Lasers

Fiber optics

Digital signaling processing

Computer hardware

Software

Data communications

Defense electronics

Superconductors

Japan

Virtually all the competitors my father looked up to in the '30s as he struggled just to survive are gone or but little engaged in today's electronic businesses which has been shaped from those surprises.

What does the future hold? Perhaps 32 (bits of) surprises and even greater challenges to adapt! Will many of today's players survive? Only those incultured with an elusive idea of, renewal, which obliges a proliferation of new, creative ideas of anticipation of the consequences of the surprises and an unstinting dedication to committing to the risk and the promise of those unchartable ideas, will thrive.

SOME OUTSIDE IDEAS

*"Thoughtlessness gets us into trouble.
Pride keeps us there."*

UNKNOWN

An American Agenda
for Private Sector Industrial Intents
and Initiatives

We, associated with business, can and should raise our expectation levels dramatically! We can build American business larger and faster. We can win a greater share of our own and foreign markets. We can create sooner a wealthier base from which we can better afford the needs of the Republic. And, thus, we can (more than incidentally) blunt a few of those imponderables — fiscal deficit and trade deficit, domestic debt and third country debt, interest rates and currency rates.

We can do this if we will only *intend it* in concrete ways by charting a course. Achieving results like larger and faster and greater shares and wealthier are not attained by default or by drifting.

I call for an American Agenda for Private Sector Industrial Intents and Initiatives.

I suggest that we can uniquely chart a course without risking the cherished principles of our private enterprise system. Yes, we might even enhance it!

The ten words of the subject — a title, if you will — will explain themselves. I make no pretext of having a clever title. Rather, each word is meant to have meaning.

It calls for:

An Agenda not directives

Private not government

Industrial meaning all business
    Manufacturing
    Commercial
    Service Industries

Intentions with private initiatives

How might we do this?

What intents might we initiate?

To implement an American Agenda of private sector industrial intents and initiatives, a Private Sector Board for Industrial Intents and Initiatives should be established by Act of Congress. The enabling legislation could be similar to the spirit behind the establishment of the private sector entities that govern the Malcolm Baldrige National Quality Award, but even more so. No powers will be vested in the government regarding the activities of the board of the intents and initiatives that it proposes.

The process of nomination and incumbency of Board members is to be decided later, but all members are to be from the private-for-profit business sector.

Proposals for possible intents and initiatives that may be accepted and acclaimed may be submitted from any private sector commercial institution.

The charter of the Board is to identify and selectively acclaim intents and initiatives deemed progressive and practical in the interest of the private sector serving its customers better. These intents may take the form of policies.

The full authority to invest in and manage the selected intents and initiatives is reserved to the individual or affiliated private sector businesses subject to current laws and regulations. With or without the acclamation by the Board of a nominated intent, any company will go about its individual goals independently as usual, of course.

Intents and initiatives under this program are limited to those for which no financial subsidy is required from the government.

The private sector may seek to persuade the public sector to endorse and facilitate certain of its intents.

If the role of the government to endorse and facilitate were to oblige incremental administration expenses and traditional (non-subsidy) services, such costs would be authorizable within the normal operating budget of the appropriate branch or department.

Let's deal with an apparent but not a real incongruity that could be misinterpretable from this introduction to the implementation plan.

Why an Act of Congress? The title says private.

Why occasional national endorsement and facilitating?

There are many justifications.

These intents often should have countrywide dimension.

They may need national visibility and standing.

We should both write the government imprimatur into the plan at the beginning so that we can simultaneously write them out of the ongoing execution.

As you will surmise from examples I am about to recite, an environment conducive to confidence building for the private investor can be enhanced for some initiatives by a national recognition and approbation of the initiatives' importance.

And now for examples.

The following are seven examples of possible intents and initiatives on the part of the private sector.

1. *Let it be the intent of all business to elevate the standards and performance of quality and productivity by a giant leap. This can be accomplished if all companies of a minimum size were to decide now, and prepare eventually, to compete for the Malcolm Baldrige National Quality Award. The private sector board should declare unto itself and urge a supporting declaration by the President that it shall be the national policy for all such companies to eventually, but early on, compete for the Malcolm Baldrige National Quality Award. It is reasonable to expect that the normal growth rate of the Gross National Product will increase by at least .5%. The reason: all the resources essential to a top quality program (R&D, processes, tools) are fundamental economic multipliers.*

2. *Let it be the intent of the nation to take the next step similar to that taken when it was decided to grid the country with railroads, wire the nation with telephone and expand transportation with a grand national highway*

system. Similarly, let it now be the intent to wire the
nation with broadband fiber optic cable for the next,
expansive generation of communications opportunities. A
national policy to effect this result could be acclaimed. The
growth benefits: value of infrastructure capital investment;
tens of billions of dollars of new services and terminals;
implement the U.S. system earlier than other countries
who are already planning to move down this learning curve
while hoping to leapfrog us.

3. *It should then be our intention to move all present televi-*
sion station licensees to a preferred band on the new cable
at no or minimum cost to such licensees. This will make
possible vastly improved video communication to, and
including, high definition television with precision stan-
dards. This will allow for the recovery of the 400 MHz of
radio frequency spectrum which is presently allocated to
over-the-air television. Most of this spectrum is by systems
and standards definition unused. The recovery of this radio
frequency spectrum will reprovide a vast R.F. media on
which science will create new electronics products and
services not presently conceivable or implementable because
of the absence of the appropriate spectrum availability. The
growth benefits: billions of dollars of yet to be anticipated
new products/services, plus a superior television service.

4. *It should be the intent of industry to have a vastly*
expanded private research and development resource. We
should establish a private research and development
laboratory of the quality and size of the Bell Labs, sup-
ported by a modest part of a percent of sales tithed from
all companies of an established size. This laboratory,

privately funded and directed, would be chartered for in-house and contracted research and development. The output of its knowledge would be licensable to American industry on a preferred basis to open private sector opportunities for the benefit of customers and society and the multiplier effect benefiting all companies.

5. A national technology roadmap should be composed, regularly updated, and the pursuit of its goals encouraged. This roadmap and its goals will ultimately trigger other interests on the part of the country that may augment the intents and initiatives program of the private sector. The nation would benefit from a National Technology Policy.

6. Industry's costs affect the values we provide our customers. Industry should acknowledge the high cost of habit forming drugs in its operation and intend to drastically reduce that tens of billions of dollars in annual cost. This is the cost of poor quality, of less than optimum productivity, and the sufferance of the medical cost burden. Industry should attack this issue head-on. Public policy should allow for industry to attack this issue head-on and thus there should be established a national policy to allow and influence private industry to test all private employees periodically with authority to dismiss any multiple offending employee who would not take advantage of counseling and medical assistance. This initiative would challenge a substantial number of people to abstinence. It would be one handle on the drug problem. Quality and productivity would be enhanced and costs reduced.

7.   *Industry should reexamine the comparative weaknesses of the American enterprise system. Yes, we are proud of our enterprise system. It has achieved noble purpose but,*

   (a) *We should take note that the Japanese system now provides the means for their industrial subparts to risk with less uncertainty and thus prepare better to outperform American companies. We must search for private sector adjustments of our system to compensate.*

   (b) *We must take note of the factors that are weakening the ability to stand for long-term objectives in a range of U.S. industries. We should examine our private sector business culture critically and constructively. We must move the common will again to the principle that the financial system exists to support the producer/service economy vs. the growing trend of the producer/service economy existing to support the financial system. Our enterprise culture is critical. When it falters, it needs to be examined. Cultures can be revitalized if we intend so and take the initiatives together. Greater tangible improvements are normally leveragable off of sounder principles and process.*

These are but examples of concrete intents. If one man can conjure seven, a hundred men may conjure 700. Many of them are bound to be good.

I suggest that if most of these seven are worthy, they have the potential of about doubling our traditional growth rate of the Gross National Product.

So there are wealth creating private sector strategies out there ready to be identified. Waiting to be debated now.

Longing to be intended now.
Most of them are probably inevitable.
But why then?
Why not now?

Note: As of publication of this book, the fundamentals of this thesis and its associated recommendations have not taken root. Time will tell if ever they contribute some influence.

The Bicentennial Celebration

In the early '70s, America's attention was drawn to the prospect of the 200th anniversary of the Declaration of Independence; an event deserving of celebration. The question was: "How does one so celebrate?"

I wondered, "Would it be appropriate to march in a parade, hold a banquet, take ads in the newspaper?, etc." But these seemed unworthy. An associated question recurred: "**What** was it that we were going to celebrate?"

Early on I was fascinated by the founding process, particularly because of the founding of our Corporation by my father. What was the Declaration of Independence but the literal preamble to the eventual founding of our nation.

It finally dawned on me in early 1975 that a promising program for the bicentennial year would be the study of the founding process of our nation. This could be fashioned into a pleasing and stimulating experience for a small grouping of our family.

Some years earlier, in the course of attending a few

meetings of the Young Presidents' Organization, Mary and I had met Martin Diamond, a Professor of the Claremont Colleges in California. Martin was the revered expert on *The Federalist Papers.* Each time that we heard him as a resource at a meeting, he spoke of important fundamental lessons derived from the early history of our country. We became friends. On a few occasions he was our guest of honor at small dinner parties at our home. At these gatherings we would oblige that the entire party focus exclusively on the early history of the country and substantially on the lessons from *The Federalist Papers.* These experiences were memorable to all.

These thoughts and memories set me to designing a preliminary agenda of topics that might make for an attractive discussion and study of the founding. The first list included the Declaration of Independence itself, the Articles of Confederation, the Constitutional Convention, the Constitution and the Bill of Rights.

With these thoughts in mind I called Martin on the phone. Our conversation went something like this: "Martin, I have been puzzled as to how a person, a family, or an institution would celebrate a bicentennial. I have concluded that a pleasing and beneficial way that our family could do so would be to engage in the study of the founding process of our country. To that end I am thinking of having an active study program that would last over six months, with some 16 members of our family, from upper high school age on up to us adults." I gave him my agenda as subject to change with possibly a six subject limit. I told him I had in mind that we would meet once a month —

probably on a first Friday night. We would plan an elegant dinner party, convening at six-thirty with refreshments. We might then start with a single-focused discussion for one hour, move directly into dinner, continue the discussion over dinner, return to the living room for after-dinner coffee and conclude our discussion at ten thirty in the evening. "What do you think about this idea for which obviously we would need some professional leadership?"

Martin's response was classic. He said, "That is exactly the way the families of the era of 200 years ago trained the youth of their family. They would hire a proctor or a tutor to continuingly engage the family in formal study and discussion. I suppose that you wish me to be your proctor for the program?" I responded: "That, indeed, was my hope and I would intend that it be professionally worthwhile if you could lead."

He was disappointed to report that he would be in New Haven at Yale for the entire scholastic year during the time when we would want to conduct our dinners in the first half of 1976. But he said, "I'm so intrigued with your idea — would you give me the opportunity to locate your proctors, and notice I say two? I instantly had in mind that you should have two inasmuch as you are going to cover such an important subject which should span *The Federalist Papers* and the Anti-Federalist Papers." I did not know there were such documents as the Anti-Federalist Papers. Martin pointed out that Herb Storing, a distinguished professor at the University of Chicago, was the preeminent scholar in that field. He thought Herb would be intrigued with our project. There was another local professor at Northern

Illinois University — Dr. Franke — who he considered renowned on *The Federalist Papers.* In short, Martin was able to reach and engage these gentlemen and the two of them and I proceeded to plan for the events of the early months of 1976.

Through the latter part of 1975, we refined the agenda to the Declaration of Independence, the Articles of Confederation, the Constitution, *The Federalist Papers,* the Anti-Federalist Papers and slavery. Martin had made the point that slavery had to be one of the six items, and clearly deserved to be the wrap-up subject as it was the most pervasive, continuing issue that impacted both the start of the country and stirred our history through the Civil War, up to the residual issues today.

The professors built an abbreviated bibliography. We duplicated extensive materials for each of the 16 members of the family. For each of the meetings I arranged to send some 30 to 50 pages of homework reading for each member of the family. Simultaneously, I launched a broadened personal reading program covering some 3,000 pages. Mary organized an excellent pattern of cocktail hour, dinner and after-dinner environment. The family came to each meeting prepared. Our professors led the discussion.

The total experience was immensely pleasing to all.

For years to come, each in different ways would query: "Can we not repeat the experience of the Declaration celebration on some other subject or event?" The information and impressions derived influenced the thinking of everyone from that time forward.

There were incidental derivatives. In the course of my

private reading, I read a book called *Forth to the Wilderness*. It was a cherished book of a friend, Bob Dille, who encouraged that I read it because it was an authentic history of those who lived in the wilds that made up most of our geography. In that book, a map was described—a map that had been completed in 1755 by a botanist-cartographer by the name of John Mitchell. The map was identified as being of considerable importance in the early history of the colonies and in the proceedings of our country after it became a nation.

I decided to look into the map and made initial inquiries, during which time I learned some of the lingo of the map collector. On an occasion when Mary and I were in London in the late '70s, I had the opportunity to visit one of London's rare book and map shops—a formal and elegant establishment. When greeted by one proprietor, I asked: "Do you have a Mitchell '55?" I had learned that one who is knowledgeable does not identify with the century, but only the years within the century. The proprietor was struck by my apparent familiarity. He identified immediately with the John Mitchell 1755 map, but had none to offer.

While he was calling friends in the trade in hopes of finding one, an American browser approached me from elsewhere in the shop and asked if I was looking for a Mitchell. He knew of one recently available, ironically, at 333 North Michigan Avenue in Chicago, my home. An excellent first edition, third folio, was located three months later and I acquired it.

It turned out that the Library of Congress adjudged

the Mitchell '55 as the most important single map in the history of our country because it was used to establish the Proclamation Line by the Lords' Commissioners of Trades and Plantations who literally managed the American colonies, helped settle the Seven Year War in 1763, defined boundaries settling the War of Independence with the Treaty of Paris of 1783, and the War of 1812, and was recently used in settling a fisheries dispute with Canada in 1932.

This started my map and ship collection — a decoration idea that was derived from these experiences. The symbolism of maps as a means of planning direction, and ships as the means of propelling and implementing our plans, became the central decorating theme of a part of our Chief Executive Office facilities.

The bicentennial celebration idea permitted our family to look back and rejoice in the founding of our country, and derived into an activating symbol of mapping out and journeying forth to our Corporate future.

The Student Dialogue

"Dear Mr. Galvin:
. . .The young man isn't mad at you; he just doesn't like you."

These words are not those of a disgruntled Motorola employee or customer. They were written by a college student about businessmen in general.

They were written in the course of a series of dialogues which I carried on with students from various colleges throughout the country.

These dialogues were part of an effort to build a better climate of understanding between the college students and us in business; part of an attempt to discover why a sizeable proportion of college students had negative attitudes toward the business world.

The fact that this attitude existed at the time of the dialogue, the late '60s, is not new or startling. It has occurred before and since. Its existence and potential effect on business motivated me to embark on a personal effort to evaluate the reasons and hopefully influence opinions.

A friend, Vern Alden, the then President of Miami University, stirred my interest. He made an emphatic case of student disenchantment, even hostility, at the time.

The vehicle I chose to communicate with the students was the Dialogue — an open letter exchange between six college men and myself. The letters were printed in college papers across the country.

In response to the Alden challenge which I embraced, the Student Dialogue idea was conceived by our Public Relations people, led by Allen Center.

The program started in the Fall of 1966. Six representative undergraduates — at Harvard, Cornell, Michigan State, University of California, University of Illinois and the University of Texas — were selected as correspondents. These young men had, for the most part, made their career choices — only one thought he **might** go into business. They were campus leaders respected by and representative of their peers. All had negative opinions about business and were willing to express them openly and candidly.

The program began with a published letter from me, posing the problem and formally inviting the students' participation as follows:

"I am genuinely concerned about recent studies which indicate that an alarming percentage of college students have no interest in pursuing careers in business. Many of these students show little respect for business and have a condescending attitude toward those who do choose it as a career.

"If you are motivated toward teaching, medicine, government or law, I say go at it eagerly...

"However, don't sell business short. If you shrug off a business career because you think it offers no excitement, no challenge, no chance for recognition or to make a meaningful contribution to society...I think you're wrong.

"...Perhaps certain students are misinformed and should be set straight. Or maybe we in business had best undertake a basic reappraisal of our way of doing things. If changes are in order, I'd like to find out.

"Let's discuss business openly...You express the views of those around you. I'll respond."

The student responses contained both the expected and the unexpected, both open criticisms and underlying themes. The profit motive was challenged as selfish. The students felt they would be bored by business. The corporate world was one they thought of as stultifying, offering minimal opportunity for personal growth or little chance to make significant contributions to society. In short, business might be all right for the other fellow, but they had more exciting, more important plans.

As the dialogues progressed, another theme emerged. To a man, students felt that one had to wait too long to make one's mark in the corporate world. Business wasn't willing to give youth a real responsibility. These were truly young men in a hurry, eager to apply and to test the fruits of their education. Their goals weren't primarily monetary; they were action-oriented. They wanted responsibility, recognition, and to feel that that their job would make a positive contribution.

The specter of the "organization man" was omnipresent.

The details of my response are not germane for this text. It empathized where appropriate, admitted need to change as required and presented the many exciting positives of business.

I wish I could say that my words gained many converts. I later learned of some. But they brought home a few points to me.

One had to do with Motorola's recruiting efforts where we naturally stress the company's leadership position in electronics — a pacemaking field in our rapidly changing technological society. I believe that some students were threatened by the very changes which we think of as challenge. Where we saw excitement, they saw complexity and confusion.

Most students had, and have, only a partially realistic view of "big business" — a view abetted by articles about sales measured in the hundreds of millions and employees measured by the tens of thousands. They have little or no idea of what business is doing in the way of decentralizing; no idea of the pacesetting managerial and administrative innovations designed to alleviate the problems connected with bigness.

These were the kind of subjects stressed in the dialogues. During the first year, we published more than 60 different letters — one third of which were from the students. The letters appeared in the college papers of the six correspondents and in papers at 23 other schools. It continued through a second year, adding a series of 10-minute dialogue-based programs broadcast over 35 campus radio stations.

That year I visited several campuses to learn and, in turn, hoped the students would learn from me.

The students were articulate, smart, concerned, quick to react, eager to learn and explore. Most of them wouldn't accept pat answers — some wouldn't accept any answers at all. They sought a personal commitment but they were afraid of being taken in — of being sold a bill of goods. This wariness extended to fields other than business. The prospective teacher knew all about the dictum of "publish or perish"; the political science major and pre-law student were aware of government's internal bureaucracy and the pitfalls in a large law firm; the budding scientist had heard some of the secrets of "grantsmanship."

Conservative in cost, the program's effects were notable. Hundreds of letters were received from other students, statesmen, businessmen and faculty members. A few were critical. Many were inquisitive. The dialogues set me to thinking more. (The original idea was having secondary effects.)

As a result of student complaints about the difficulties involved in finding meaningful summer jobs, Motorola reevaluated its summer internship program, trying to see to it that every job carried real responsibility and gave the young man or woman a better picture of corporate life.

Similarly, we looked at training programs, putting ourselves in the new employee's shoes to gauge his and her reactions to the first and second year of corporate life. We've been trying to build experience that will encourage creative, independent efforts and which will mark and reward ability and talent. At the same time we have pointed up the fact that in many situations there just is no substitute for experience.

We hoped other companies would take up the dialogues energetically in their own way. I didn't think we in business could convince students to care about us until we showed better that we cared about them. However, other companies did not follow a similar form of student and campus communication.

Nevertheless, various communications naturally have occurred by many, and probably sufficiently. Moods have moderated. We're pleased we had the idea and made the formal effort then. In less intense and more informal ways of campus visitations, some dialogue continues.

The Word Game

I invented a game. It's called "Your Most Important Word."

Imagine a small dinner party with six or eight of you sitting around the table. The conditions and people feel right to you. You ask for their attention.

"I'd like to suggest we play a game. It's fun. It's easy. It's stimulating. It's called — Your Most Important Word. In a moment I'm going to ask each of us to state one word. Not two. Just one. Please, no questions. Just prepare to present one word for our collective attention. This is not a contest or a test. In this game all words are created equal. If it's your most important word then for all of us it is a most important word. As improbable as it is, if the person before you utters the word you have in mind, you must promptly choose another."

Then you select the first person to contribute the first word and proceed around the table. With all the words on the open record you are in a position to commence a lively, interesting conversation.

Although neither you nor another should presume to be an overt discussion leader, you will likely find it helpful to return to the first contributor or an unusually curious attention-getting word and invite its person to put that word in play.

"Your word—love or trust or freedom or money or ?—is special. Why is it so special to you?" His or her comments almost certainly will be brief. Then ask a second person similarly. If one person's word is an opposite or complementary, it may be a particularly appropriate next choice. Once each one has given meaning to his or her word, you are off and running. The conversation will take on a life and style and vitality of its own. Typically, it can occupy the entire dining period. Occasionally extra key words later will find their way into the discussion, often usefully.

Each time you play the game it will be different. It is not likely that you will play the game with the same people frequently or ever again.

A variation of the game, however, makes repeating the process with a prior group potentially appealing. Focus on a subject—a category. Once, a group of us playing together for a second time responded to and discussed "What is your most important word concerning the Soviet Union?" The timing was uniquely appropriate as the dissolution of that crumbling empire was front page.

On another occasion I adapted the game to a joint dinner of 20—about half of us from Japan and the balance from the U.S. That occasion needed a stimulator. The group willingly gave me their attention and then responded to the introductory question, "What is your most important word re Japan-U.S. relations?" As was anticipated, only a short centralized discussion followed the tabling of the 20 words, but the ice was broken, the individual discussions enlivened and certain of the nominated words became the themes for the closing ceremonial toasts.

The game occasionally leads to surprising secondary effects. A dear lady friend said her most important word was trust. Her husband, knowing with her of her terminal illness, was moved to acquire for her a veritable art treasure from the Orient — an extraordinary calligraphy of the word trust which she especially cherished for her precious remainder years.

A 15-year-old grandson curiously selected the word automobile. He explained he hoped to found a car company someday. Imagine the discussion that ensued from that. The next night, fortuitously, he and I had dinner alone and he proceeded to impress me with his instinctive knowledge of what it would take to succeed.

You cannot be sure where the word game will lead. But it will lead somewhere.

SPECIAL IDEAS

Bob's father was genuinely interested in the outcome of his first high school inter-scholastic basketball game. "You say you did your part. You scored eleven of your team's fifty-five points. Good, and you won?" When Bob replied that the team didn't, he dutifully pronounced, "Then you didn't do all of your part."

PAUL GALVIN

New Ventures, New Enterprises, New...

Occasionally, I tease some new conversation partners with the claim that there is one best class of people. After feeding their dismay for but a moment I respond, "The founders." Founders of schools or cities or businesses or hospitals, et al. The founder provides the platform and momentum to the rest of us. The admiration for my father — our founder — can be read into that innocent but instructive verbal twist.

It is natural that other similar meanings would coexist in our institution. Renewal has been viewed continuingly as our driving thrust. Refounding, starting a new business within the established divisions, is a word that we use and act on from time to time.

The majority of new companies in the U.S. are founded by individuals who leave their prior employer and replicate a variation of the former employer's business or commence a relevant skill product/market initiative that was not supported by the prior employer. There are all manner of mostly favorable motivations for such actions.

A goodly number of these entrepreneurial initiatives effected through employee separating from prior employer should be unnecessary. Such a process can be the least optimum way to achieve the valid reward and motivations of the founder-to-be while representing opportunities to the originally employing corporation.

Established companies should be creative and hospitable in siring newly foundable prospects from within.

In the essay *The **Total** of Customer Satisfaction* on page 67, I offer an aggressive idea of how to drive the company to the most deliberate culture and process of identifying and acting to renew and blanket every relevant-to-its-area-of-interest market potential.

In addition, Motorola has identified with the idea of establishing new, new businesses. In the 1970s we instituted a deliberate activity called New Ventures. Its charter focused on opportunities within our span of competences but diverse from a direct derivative of our established businesses. It invited any of our current people to champion a latent but suppressed opportunity. A few businesses were started. Two have survived. However, we and their able leaders could not justify that either could grow sufficiently and thus remain in Motorola. Their founders bought the business which they have ably sustained.

New Ventures was my idea. It did not work out to the benefit of the corporation. Those who shepherded and invested themselves in it did their jobs well. My concept was flawed.

The worth of the idea of a greenhouse within seems fundamentally sound. 3M, in particular, is exemplary.

In the 1980s I decided to try again. A new team conceived of a substantially more appealing and promising formation. It deserved a new name — the simple signification — New Enterprises. A primary difference between the prior and the new was our intention in the '80s program to **actively** identify arenas of markets and products relevant to our competences and **actively** recruit the leadership inside or out. Motorola provided all the other resources. The original Venture program was mostly passive — an environment and process and resourcing entity available to be claimed. The new program called for positive corporate initiatives. The equity reward potential in each was similar.

The New Enterprise version of a business greenhouse is more promising. Many of the entrepreneurs and stewards of this program have more than fulfilled their particular personal responsibilities. They have persevered and we have the long view. Prospects continue for notable success from among the present New Enterprise businesses. Good work is evident. Patience and perseverance is likely to pay off.

The achievement of the more promising businesses would initiate a track record around which others could strengthen the system. But in important ways we are still searching for the formula and instinct to add the final increment of success to the overall New Enterprise process. The substance of my idea is at least incomplete. Others may yet make it whole.

If a refined and dynamic New Enterprise activity can earn credentials, it will add a giant distinctive competence to the institution, Motorola. Few established companies have or ever will achieve a new, new enterprising competence. We can attest to the elusiveness of the objective. But as inadequate as I have been in formulating the winning idea and plan, I am convinced it is doable.

New Enterprises is an idea that may still need another idea. The two may finally do.

Reporting Profits

There is a better idea for reporting profits. It's an idea I have fostered for decades. It has not been adopted by others. Obviously, it is at least unpopular, if not, less than adequate.

Typically, profits are reported as a rate of change. Headlines and lead sentences state: "Profits soared 70% compared to"; "Earnings sink 40% from...." Compared to what?

Readers and listeners rarely have the time or the inclination to relate the superficial headline to base data. The prior period may have been a management disaster, but today we celebrate a 70% improvement from virtually nothing. The prior quarter may have been a giant success. The 40% reduction merely returned us closer to our already high profit standard. What casual reader/listener (which includes most of us) is fundamentally better informed by this repetitive, insufficient, noninterpretable — mostly misinterpretable — PR?

Quarter after quarter newspapers and radio and video media are filled predominantly with rate of change percentages and adjectives that propagandize all manner of heightened or lessened earnings. Those who read the upbeat can have a warm feeling; those who read the downbeat can have a sinking feeling. Such headlined information is of little substantive use and has contributed to a counter-productive consequence.

Such information creates the counter-productive mindset for the non-concentrating reader and listener, so many of whom are also insufficiently informed on the realistic relative "numbers" in business. Exaggerated adjectives and high percent of change numbers conjure the image of a business system that has excessive profits. More often than not, readers and listeners hearing rate of change numbers like 40% and 60% actually interpret that those are the rates of earnings. Even when the numbers speak of major decreases the same mindset is reenforced. Readers can question: if profits can fluctuate that much they must have the potential of being too large in the first place.

Both for the reason of improving the public image and the understanding by the vast majority of readers and listeners, I have been an advocate of the idea of headlining profits primarily as the percent of net margin and not rate of change. There are other options, but this is the most universally relevant number.

Were that to be the culture, the habit, the standard, then the headlines would read more as follows: "Company A's profits increase to 4.9%; Company B's profits fall to 2.3%." Occasionally there will be reporting of uniquely successful companies whose actual profit net margins are in the double digits. But for the most part the reading and hearing of net margin data would more accurately report a useful key fact and establish in the minds of all observers that the typical rates of profit in business range near 3%, 4%, 5% or 6%. Of course we can then additionally deal intelligently with rates of change if one wishes to compare, for example, a margin of 4% one year to an improvement to 5% the next.

Admittedly, this would take sizzle out of the headlines of business pages. But business pages should not be aiming for artificial sizzle. Admittedly, many chief executive officers who have suffered their own poor performance in one reporting period will not be able to relish reading about their company's improvement from a poor 2% net margin to a still insignificant 3% net margin by not headlining that they have made a 50% improvement in earnings. Fuller, more balanced, yet telegraphable accurate information and correct perceptions should be of high order for public relations purposes of business and the business press.

I identified this idea early on in my career and Motorola's public announcements have not since contained any volunteered rate of change representation regarding earnings. Ironically, editors instantly calculate, and rate of change more often than not becomes the prominent lead text of their report. Human nature being what it is, it is probable that this idea will not become popular. But I respectfully suggest that business and the business press are passing up a valuable tool in conveying to all of the publics what should be the fuller and correct information and image of earnings.

What Might Have Been

Two ideas, unfulfilled, could have made a difference in the destiny of the company and a bit of the world. Whether for the good or less is now but a matter of others' speculation.

The first: Broadcasting. Television station ownership in the U.S.

The second: A semiconductor partnership with the Swiss watch industry early on.

~

My father brilliantly and courageously positioned and led the company to a major share of the television receiver market in the U.S. at the birth of the industry, shortly after World War II. As this strategy was initially unfolding, I went to him with a complementary idea. Enter television broadcasting.

The chicken/egg dilemma was an issue of genuine concern. As a television set manufacturer, my father looked straight through that uncertainty, gambling that superior value product would move well in enough markets in the founding years.

The uncertainty dilemma delayed aggressive quests by others for station licenses in many of the upper-tiered second markets like Atlanta, St. Louis and one of our new corporate home towns, Phoenix. I urged that we file for, own and operate five of those class of market licenses both to seed the demand for sets via early programming and for the long run prospect of lucrative advertising income from the market-by-market oligopoly that was destined for each territory due to the limited licenses. Considering the size and resources of the company in the late-'40s, each strategy individually was close to a bet-your-company risk.

My father's confidence in equipment sales was substantial. The company's modest size but steady, proven track record supported it. But, obviously, that confidence could not be unqualified.

The prospect for television stations having to bear some, if not many, years of market development investment and cost before turning a profit had to be assumed. The aggregate risk was more than he thought justified. He turned the broadcasting idea down.

I respected the decision. His choice was the pivotable idea. The television equipment business thrived for years and helped nourish the growing communication business and the fledgling semiconductor business through the '50s.

A case can be made that both of the strategies might have been digestible. As a matter of fact, most stations broke even on an early vs. a late time scale. Had we taken that gamble, it is likely (in hindsight) it would have been affordable. The financial fortunes of the company in the '60s and '70s would have been uncommonly richer. In that era, stations earned high double-digit profit margins and would have contributed a multiple of available monetary resources for product R&D and capital equipment for many product and systems opportunities.

But other questions are left to ponder. If we had committed to stations, would we have taken a weaker stance for semiconductors in the mid-'50s? If we would have enjoyed the disproportionate rewards of the golden years of TV broadcasting, would it have softened our resolve for our other businesses? Would we have been able to grow the talent for show business? Would it have been as much fun? The fact is, the company did what it did successfully and has become what it has become. I have never questioned or regretted the decision. The voice of experience, my father's, was right then. That's what mattered. Sometimes a good idea like broadcasting is not best.

~

By 1960, our semiconductor business was standing on its own two feet in the U.S. We had to start looking to the Far East and Western Europe. Dan Noble had set the course in solid state. His, our associates and my objectives and thirst for world share and success, drove Dan and I jointly to Europe and Japan frequently.

The Europe study revealed a unique opportunity — the electronic watch. While our principal objectives were the even more extensive communications, consumer, computer, automotive, etc., applications of transistors and integrated circuits, the horological — timekeeping — applications were challenging and promising. The Swiss dominated the market then with well-honed mechanical movements and analog displays (standard hour and minute hand dials). The prospect of electronic circuitry with digital displays was apparent but not yet satisfyingly reproducible. The threat of the new to the old was obvious. The emergent ambitions of Japan and Hong Kong were not to be ignored.

Together, Dan and I made special trips to Switzerland to learn about the industry and the companies and the leaders and the significance of their relationships to each other through their associations. Modest effort was already under way by them to understand and prepare for the prospective technology discontinuity.

From our vantage point, their effort was complacent and insufficient. If the Swiss industry was to control its electronic product destiny it would have to embrace a sense of urgency and the principle of partnership with a semiconductor company of competence and substantial size. The watch industry volume alone would not afford the varied and challenging forecastable electronics developments.

We eventually proposed that we were that best-in-class partner, moving rapidly to the size and capability that their various end-product companies could develop around and depend on, just as the various great Swiss brand names depended on the specialist, mechanical parts manufacturers and movement assemblers for their traditional products.

For our part we envisioned tying a special engineering and factory operation at the French/Swiss border into our other planned continental semiconductor operations. The Swiss industry could joint venture with us there, thus providing advanced, dedicated design and supply resources.

Most of the influential Swiss whom we had come to know found it difficult to believe that electronics would be unduly revolutionary and if it were to be so eventually, they leaned to "in-house" or at least "all European" response which they assumed to be achievable. Their self-sufficiency over centuries bred a befogged overconfidence. A presumption of need for an American supplier was hard to embrace. Obviously, Dan and I could neither sell the need for the Swiss to jointly and vigorously influence the new technology nor sell our competence to play a key role in Swiss integration into it.

With concerted effort could the two entities have set the electronic watch standards with attendant continuing Swiss market leadership in the new watch? Would the overwhelming surge from the Far East have been blunted? It, at least, was within our private enterprising, combined and respective powers to have tried. Regrettably, their private interests held back.

It was not long before the Swiss substantially defaulted that product and we went on as planned to successfully resource for the other major volume semiconductor markets elsewhere in Europe.

Ironically, for different trade policy reasons, we were not welcome to supply the same emerging potential in Japan at that time either so we shortly redirected our watch component resources to the other semiconductor markets.

The right pivotable ideas are critical in response to discontinuities. Without them one cannot dare to achieve. What might have been had we engaged in these dares?

*Where Would We Be Today **If**?*

Where would we be today if the following dozen illustrative key ideas were not conceived and risked by the early- and mid-year pioneers of the company?

1. *Paul Galvin was driven by a compulsive idea: be in business for himself. A Ph.D in management would never have entered the B Battery Eliminator business in 1928. Irony of ironies, the dumbest of ideas was the most determinative. We were born!*
2. *Once the hint of a possibility of a radio in a car was grasped from others' early custom applications, the idea of a standard, reproducible design was pivotal. So simple, in retrospect. But not all that common in the late-'20s. At least no one else thought of it.*
3. *The key company players dreamt up the marriage of a receiver and transmitter in a hand-holdable package, the Army SCR 536 hand-held portable radio, pre-World War II. And incidentally, they tasted the future of the commer-*

cial two-way radio market. They probably should not have afforded it at the time.

4. They saw the difference that Frequency Modulation — FM — would make for land mobile communications while others pondered Amplitude Modulation too long.

5. They understood that communications customers always wanted to talk farther than the specifications prescribed. While other would-be competitors of the new land mobile radio business designed to cost and spec, our people designed to optimum performance and the customers followed us out beyond the expected limits of reception and beyond our early dreams of success.

6. Those customers wanted sure installation and maintenance, so we chose the unconventional — sell and service direct. Critical, different from others' ideas.

7. Paging. People take it for granted today. Motorola conceived the system and had the perseverance to overcome years of market apathy.

8. The volume commitment to low-priced TV in the founding year of television was an idea that surprised every competitor and put Motorola in the major league of the 1950s home electronics industry.

9. The idea to risk entering semiconductor manufacturing and electing to go full bore in the merchant market was seminal.

10. Motorola's ideas regarding alternators, power generators for cars, built around our distinctive power semiconductors, revolutionized the entire worldwide automotive industry, obliging it to convert from positive ground to negative ground electrical systems forevermore.

11. *Cellular mobile telephone was conceived as early at Motorola as anywhere, promulgated more aggressively and would not have been marketable for years later than its actual introduction without Motorola's aggressive public advocacies and a myriad of Motorola unequaled system and component innovations.*
12. *Japan, as competitor and market, conjured a maze of ideas springing from the company's strategic drive.*

~

These and other legendary ideas are vital to our corporate history. They are striking.

The most striking literary legends that testify to the power of creative thinking are the wonderous tales of **Scheherazade** throughout those thousand and one Arabian nights. You will recall that she was to be disposed of by her untrusting husband, the all powerful King of Sassan, the day following their marriage. She enticed him into believing that she had so stirring a story to extol that she should be spared to regale him at least a second night. Fascinated by her intriguing adventures of Sinbad and baited by her hint that a sequel was even more exciting, he postponed her sentence again and again as she invented the likes of the Lamp and Ali Baba.

Each night she stretched her imagination and did so a thousand times over until the royal monarch succumbed to her uncommon and entertaining genius, which earned her his trusting and lasting love.

The challenge to the creative thinking of our people is the test of reality vs. fiction. The fresh and renewing sequels we must conjure and bring to life determine our sustained and growing acceptance with our King — the customer.

In our case the "thousand" relates to thousands of people who have had multithousands of ideas that have made and sustained this company. Where will we be tomorrow if thousands of our people do not have and act on more than our share of the better of these classes of new ideas?

About the Author and Motorola

Motorola was founded in 1928 by Paul Galvin as the Galvin Manufacturing Co. He led and built the company until 1959.

The author, Robert Galvin, his son, began with the company in 1940, shared the chief executive office in the '50s, and headed the company from 1959 to 1990.

At the time of publication of the book, Bob Galvin is Chairman of the Executive Committee of Motorola, Inc., a full-time officership responsibility. Motorola as of this time employs 107,000 people worldwide, with yearly sales over $13 billion. All of its products and services — communications, computers, controls and components — are electronics-based.